(4)

S0-BEP-410

Colorado Bucket List Adventure Guide

Explore 100 Offbeat Destinations You Must Visit!

Don Harris

Bridge Press
support@bridgepress.org

Please consider writing a review!
Just visit: purplelink.org/review

Copyright 2021. Bridge Press. All Rights Reserved.
No part of this book may be reproduced or transmitted in any form or
by any means, electronic or mechanical, including photocopying,
recording or by any other form without written permission from the
publisher.

ISBN: 978-1-955149-44-0

FREE BONUS

Discover 31 Incredible Places You Can
Visit Next! Just Go to:

purplelink.org/travel

Table of Contents

Denver

Dillon

Dinosaur

Divide

Durango

How to Use This Book

Welcome to your very own adventure guide to exploring the many wonders of the state of Colorado. Not only does this book lay out the most wonderful places to visit and sights to see in the vast state, but it also provides driving directions and GPS Coordinates for Google Maps to make exploring that much easier.

Adventure Guide
Sorted by region, this guide offers over 100 amazing wonders found in Colorado for you to see and explore. These can be visited in any order, and this book will help you keep track of where you've been and where to look forward to going next. Each entry describes the area or place, what to look for, how to get there, and what you may need to bring along. Listed fees are accurate as of the publication date but may be subject to change.

GPS Coordinates
As you can imagine, not all the locations in this book have a physical address. Fortunately, some of our listed wonders are either found within a national park or reserve, or are near a city, town, or place of business. For those that are not associated with a specific location, it is easiest to map it using GPS coordinates.

Luckily, Google has a system of codes that converts the coordinates into pin drop locations that Google Maps is able to interpret and navigate.

Each adventure in this guide will include both the GPS coordinates and general directions on how to find the location.

It is important that you are prepared for poor cell signals. To work around this, pre-route your destination and save the directions for use offline. Depending on your device and the distance of some locations, you may need to travel with a backup battery source.

About Colorado

It took 100 years after the signing the Declaration of Independence for Colorado to earn its statehood, and it may take you that long to explore everything hidden in the Great Plains, mountain ranges, ski resorts, state parks, and trailheads scattered throughout the Centennial State.

Colorado was founded at the turn of the 19th century as a critical piece of the Louisiana Purchase. However, Native Americans inhabited the area for nearly 13,000 years before Spain and the United States claimed the land.

No matter where you explore, the history of Colorado will be there to greet you every step of the way. People wishing to explore the wilds and wildernesses of the Americas have traversed them for thousands of years. To this day, hikers can still find remnants and artifacts from those who inhabited the area as early as 11,000 BCE.

While the Southern Rocky Mountains are the most recognizable, there is more to Colorado than just one mountain range. From the cave dwellings in Mesa Verde State Park to the petroglyphs at the Dinosaur National Monument, from the historic hot springs at Orvis to the man-made ice climbs at Ouray, there are centuries of culture, history, flora, and fauna to feast your eyes on.

Landscape and Climate

Colorado is home to the highest peaks in the Rocky Mountains, juxtaposed with vast, sweeping views of the Great Plains. Made up of the Middle and Southern Rocky mountain ranges, the latter of which contains the famous Pikes Peak, the Colorado landscape also includes the Wyoming Basin and the Colorado Plateau.

Despite the mountainous landscape, Colorado is relatively quiet when it comes to seismic activity, and earthquakes are rare. However, the plains are subject to tornadoes and flash flooding during the spring, and avalanches are always a risk when hiking or camping in the peaks.

Colorado boasts one of the most diverse climates in the country. With one part Great Plains and one part Rocky Mountain Range—and a bit of desert thrown in—the weather is less predictable and less temperate than other mountainous states.

Southern Colorado is not much warmer than the northern parts of the state, and snow can stay on the mountains well into the summer. Weather will change drastically as you climb in elevation, so pack appropriately if you plan on visiting the foothills or climbing up to the top of Pikes Peak.

Fortunately, a diverse climate leads to more adventure. The wildlife and local wildflowers can differ depending on the part of the state you're in and the season you plan to visit. While the state is open all year round, the climate will impact the types of activities you can do. But as long as you bring the right shoes for the weather, hiking the trails across the peaks or plains is always an option.

Fort Garland

During the mid-1800s, the fort was one of the first people would see when crossing into the territory headed west. Today, Fort Garland is still a quaint stop on your way to the Great Sand Dunes National Park. The fort itself is now a museum and cultural center where visitors can walk in the footsteps of the early pioneers. Tour five adobe buildings belonging to the original 19th-century fort, one of which is converted into an art and history exhibit, and learn more about the Ute Tribe, Buffalo Soldiers, and early settlers in the area. The city of Fort Garland provides local campsites and connects visitors to campgrounds in the Rio Grande National Forest and Sangre de Cristo Wilderness Area. Enjoy hiking, camping, birdwatching, and wildlife here. Time permitting, animal lovers should visit the nearby Alamosa and Monte Vista National Wildlife Refuges.

Best Time to Visit: June, July, August

Pass/Permit/Fees: The Fort Garland Museum and Cultural Center costs $5 per adult, $4.50 per senior, and $3.50 per student. Children under 6 are free.

Closest City or Town: Alamosa

How to Get There: From Denver, take US-160 E for 24.5 miles, and then turn left onto Pfeiffer Ave. Turn right at the first cross street onto 5th avenue to reach Fort Garland.

GPS Coordinates: 37.4289° N, -105.4339° W

Did You Know? Famous Wild West settler Kit Carson commanded Fort Garland and successfully negotiated a treaty with the Ute tribe in 1867.

Great Sand Dunes National Park

The unique sand formations in Great Sand Dunes National Park are created by the wind patterns within the San Luis Valley of the Sangre de Cristo Mountains. It's home to the largest sandbox and the highest mountains of sand in the country. Hiking, picnics, and camping abound, but everyone loves a sled ride down the slippery dunes. Campers willing to carry all of their gear with them can enjoy free access to backcountry campsites.

Backpacking is encouraged (with a permit), especially on the Sand Ramp Trail, which leads to the mountains. Wheelchair-accessible paths are available, and special sand wheelchairs are offered with a reservation. Hiking through the park at sunset is a must. When night falls, don't forget to look up at the sky honeycombed with stars.

Best Time to Visit: May through September. May is the best time to see the snow runoff that streams down the mountains and across the sands.

Pass/Permit/Fees: $25 for up to 6 passengers, $40 for up to 25, or $100 for 26 or more.

Closest City or Town: Alamosa

How to Get There: From Alamosa, take US-160 E toward Fort Garland, then CO-150 N. From Colorado Springs, head south on I-25 to US-160 W, then CO-150 N.

GPS Coordinates: 37.7275° N, -105.6418° W

Did You Know? The Great Sand Dunes National Park was named an International Dark Sky Park in 2019.

Ouzel Falls

If you're looking for a day hike, head to Ouzel Falls. Nothing beats the views, and hikers are treated to three more cascade waterfalls on their way up to the 40-foot falls. You'll reach Ouzel Falls via the Wild Basin Trail. Access the trailhead by Highway 115 right outside Allenspark, but be aware that the highway is a dirt road. Bad weather will make it near to impossible for vehicles without four-wheel drive to pass.

Weather permitting, the 5-mile round trip at Ouzel Falls leads to Copeland and Lower Copeland Falls as well as Calypso Cascades. You'll reach the first waterfall within the first half-mile. Slip onto the parallel path at St. Vrain Creek to get a closer look and then hop back on the trailhead without having to backtrack.

Best Time to Visit: Late spring when the melting snow turns the falls into something beautiful

Pass/Permit/Fees: $25 per vehicle or $15 per pedestrian

Closest City or Town: Allenspark

How to Get There: From Allenspark, take CO-7 W to County Rd. 84. Turn right onto CO-115 to reach the falls in 2.2 more miles.

GPS Coordinates: 40.1989° N, -105.6011° W

Did You Know? If you can handle another 7 miles, hikers can bask in the view of Bluebird Lake and its wildflowers in the spring.

Peak to Peak Scenic Byway

If you don't stop, it will only take you about 90 minutes to drive the Peak to Peak Scenic Byway, but we dare you not to stop at least once. Between the Indian Peaks Wilderness Area, the Arapaho and Roosevelt National Forests, and the historical sites in Estes Park, Central City, and more, it's going to be hard to stay in the car. During the mild months, stop along the byway to fish in the Gross Reservoir, or reserve a campsite in the Indian Peaks near Ward. In the winter, stop off and explore the ghost towns of Apex, Hesse, and Nevadaville, which were once some of the wealthiest mining cities. We recommend giving yourself 2–3 hours to drive Peak to Peak Byway, stopping wherever you want along the way. From the rugged outdoors to American history, there's something on this scenic byway for everyone.

Best Time to Visit: Any time of year is a perfect time to drive, but September and October show off the forests' fall foliage.

Pass/Permit/Fees: The byway is free to drive.

Closest City or Town: Allenspark

How to Get There: From Allenspark, head north on Ski Rd. to CO-7 W. Turn left onto CO-7 W, and in 14.8 miles, you'll reach the byway.

GPS Coordinates: 40.3752° N, -105.5096° W

Did You Know? Central City used to be the richest square mile in the country during the mining peak of the 19th century.

Independence Pass

Independence Pass is the highest point of Colorado's scenic and historic byways, reaching over 12,000 feet above sea level at its pinnacle. The drive is a little over 30 miles long, leading visitors on a narrow path carved into the side of the Rocky Mountains. You'll pass through the famous ghost town of Independence, the San Isabel National Forest, and the White River National Forest. Luckily, there are plenty of pull-offs, overlooks, and campsites for anyone who wants to get out and savor the view.

It will take 45 minutes to drive the pass without stopping, but you should carve out extra time to really take in the scenery. Get out at the Grottos Day Use Area for a picnic and easy hiking trails that lead to waterfalls, an ice cave, and the Devil's Punch Bowl. More difficult hiking trails lie ahead, leading to the mining ghost town of Ruby and Roaring Fork.

Best Time to Visit: The pass is open from Memorial Day to early November.

Pass/Permit/Fees: None

Closest City or Town: Aspen

How to Get There: From Aspen, follow CO-82 E/E. Cooper Ave. for 19.3 miles to reach the pass.

GPS Coordinates: 39.0186° N, -106.5640° W

Did You Know? Independence is named after miners who struck gold in the Roaring Fork Valley on July 4, 1879.

Maroon Bells

The Maroon Bells in the Elk Mountains are the two most photographed peaks in Colorado. Both Maroon Peak and North Maroon Peak are just over 14,000 feet high and surrounded by a natural reflection lake. Take the mile-long Maroon Lake Scenic Trail around the lake, or choose a longer hike on either the Maroon Creek Trail (6.5 miles) or Crater Lake Trail (3.6 miles). The Maroon Bells are part of the White River National Forest, giving visitors ample opportunity to hike and explore other trails in the wilderness, including the Four Pass Loop and Conundrum Trail. The latter leads to Conundrum Hot Springs, a popular camping destination. Access to the peaks is restricted during the winter, but hikers can still cross-country ski, snowshoe, or ride snowmobiles.

Best Time to Visit: Any time before June or after September will have fewer crowds.

Pass/Permit/Fees: $10 per vehicle, parking available at $15 for 8 hours

Closest City or Town: Aspen

How to Get There: From Aspen, head south on N. Galena St. and turn right onto E. Main St. Take another right onto N. 7th St. Turn left onto CO-82 W. At the traffic circle, take the second exit onto Maroon Creek Rd. In 9.4 miles, you will find the Maroon Bells.

GPS Coordinates: 39.0708490° N, -106.9889920° W

Did You Know? Mudstone gives the Maroon Bells their unique reddish color.

Maroon Lake Scenic Trail

This is one of the most accessible hiking trails in Colorado. Most of Maroon Lake Scenic Trail is paved except for the upper portion, and all of it is wheelchair accessible. For a more challenging hike, take the 4-mile trailhead to Crater Lake. No matter where you decide to hike (or camp), the views of the Maroon Bells are breathtaking. Plan on backpacking? Make sure to get the appropriate permits from the Forest Service. The Maroon Lake Scenic Trail is a rite of passage for any Colorado local, and many visitors take to the trail during the summer and the fall. Personal vehicles are prohibited from accessing the path during the peak season, but there is a shuttle bus service that leaves from the Aspen Highlands Village every twenty minutes. The shuttle stops at 5 p.m., so plan accordingly.

Best Time to Visit: Visit before fall, as roads leading to the trail are closed by October and through the winter.

Pass/Permit/Fees: A bus pass is $6 for adults and $4 for children.

Closest City or Town: Aspen

How to Get There: From Aspen, follow CO-82 W, and at the traffic circle, take the second exit onto Maroon Creek Rd. Continue on Maroon Creek Rd. for 9.3 miles, and turn left to reach the Maroon Lake Trailhead.

GPS Coordinates: 39.0967° N, -106.9451° W

Did You Know? Aggressive moose live near the trail, and portions of your hike may be blocked off.

Boreas Pass Road

Pack for a road trip and head to Breckenridge. You'll hit Boreas Pass Scenic Route, a 60-minute ride from Breckenridge to Como that tours through an awe-inspiring alpine drive. It climbs over 11,000 feet up with stunning views of the Tenmile Range and Continental Divide.

The drive is short enough to be a day trip from Denver or Aspen, and drivers have plenty of time to visit nearby ghost towns and outdoor museums along the way.

Take any chance to get out of the car for a breath of fresh air or to stretch your legs. Biking and hiking trails for all skill levels line the pass, and campers are welcome to explore the numerous sites down from the road. Summit County provides a 15-campsite space if you want to stay overnight, but it's first come, first served.

Best Time to Visit: Summer. The pass is closed from October to May.

Pass/Permit/Fees: Free to drive

Closest City or Town: Breckenridge

How to Get There: From Breckenridge, use County Rd. 503 to reach Boreas Pass Rd.

GPS Coordinates: 39.4111° W, -105.9694° N

Did You Know? Until 1938, Boreas Pass was the highest narrow-gauge railway in the country.

Vail Ski Resort

Vail Ski Resort is the largest ski resort in Colorado, which isn't surprising given that Vail itself was founded as a ski resort in 1966. Since then, the city has grown to accommodate the thousands of annual visitors who come every winter. Luckily, skiing isn't the only thing in Vail anymore. Summer events fill the calendar, and Vail offers outdoor events for the whole family all season long. Take to the slopes without the snow on a 330-foot tubing hill, or hold on for dear life on the Alpine Coaster. Biking, hiking, and backpacking abound on the many trails in the city, including the easy 2-mile Meadow Loop up to the 3-mile Berry Picker Trail that takes you 2,200 feet up. Climb your own way up the mountain, or start your hike with a scenic ride in Vail's two gondolas.

Best Time to Visit: The ski season is December through March.

Pass/Permit/Fees: None, but Vail is one of the most expensive cities in Colorado.

Closest City or Town: Breckenridge

How to Get There: From Breckenridge, get on I-70 W and take Exit 176 toward Vail. At the traffic circle, take the fourth exit onto Vail Rd. At the next traffic circle, take the third exit onto Frontage Rd. E. Take a slight right onto Vail Valley Dr. to reach the ski resort.

GPS Coordinates: 39.6403° N, -106.3742° W

Did You Know? Vail Mountain was originally known as Shining Mountain.

Boulder Museum of Contemporary Art

Three galleries of national, international, and local modern art fill the Boulder Museum. The museum was founded by a group of Boulder artists in 1972 to educate audiences of all ages on the importance of art in our time.

Unique exhibitions in the past have included Emilio Lobato's paper airplanes and the pensive journey of Caroline Douglas's clay creatures. Exhibits often feature multiple artists curated by the museum's talented team, but some only stick around for a month or so. Other exhibits may stay for an entire season, and planning ahead is the only way to guarantee you see the artist you want. Nearby, you can explore downtown Boulder, including Central Park and the Boulder County Farmers Market on select days.

Best Time to Visit: April through November is the best time to visit.

Pass/Permit/Fees: $2 for adults, seniors, students, and educators

Closest City or Town: Boulder

How to Get There: In Boulder, head west on Arapahoe Ave., then turn right on 14th St. and left on 13th St. The museum is on the right at 1750 13th St.

GPS Coordinates: 40.0152° N, -105.2774° W

Did You Know?
The museum store is a curated shop all its own, featuring art and jewelry from local artists.

Boulder Reservoir

Boulder Reservoir was completed in 1955 as a water storage facility for northern Colorado and the city of Boulder, but it moonlights today as a playground for locals and tourists alike. Fishing, boating, and swimming are among the most popular activities, and there are plenty of opportunities to sail and windsurf in the summer. In the winter, take out a pole for ice fishing. Maybe you'll catch a rainbow trout or smallmouth bass. Swimmers should be aware that the swimming area is only open from May until August, and anyone under 13 must pass a swim test.

Not ready to get your feet wet? Stay dry on the 5.3-mile Boulder Reservoir Loop Trail. Look out for wildlife, including raptors and other birds, snakes, prairie dogs, deer, and rabbits.

Best Time to Visit: The reservoir is beautiful all year round, but there are more events in winter and summer.

Pass/Permit/Fees: $7 per adult, $3.50 per child, $4.75 per senior

Closest City or Town: Boulder

How to Get There: From Boulder, take the Foothills Pkwy. to Jay Rd. Turn right on 51st St., and Reservoir Rd. will be on the right.

GPS Coordinates: 40.0737° N, -105.2370° W

Did You Know? Boulder Reservoir is part of the Colorado-Big Thompson Project that supplies water to over 1 million Colorado residents.

Celestial Seasonings Tea Factory

Famously known for its elaborate tea box art, Celestial Seasonings offers tours of its art gallery and tea factory at its Boulder location every day. Bask in the aroma of your favorite tea flavors while you enjoy a delicious home-cooked breakfast or brunch on site. Celestial Seasonings got its start in a small barn right here in Boulder, and the tour provides an inside look at the history of the tea factory, including a closer look at how its hand-sewn muslin tea bags are made. For the tea connoisseur, take a look around the Mint Room and Celestial Herb Garden.

Best Time to Visit: The factory is open all year round, and tours are offered daily from 10 a.m. to 4 p.m. On Sundays, tours are available from 11 a.m. to 3 p.m.

Pass/Permit/Fees: None. Tours are free, but you must call ahead for availability.

Closest City or Town: Boulder

How to Get There: In Boulder, head east on Arapahoe Ave. to get onto Foothills Pkwy. Take a right onto Jay Rd., left onto Spine Rd., and left onto Sleepytime Dr. to reach the factory at 4600 Sleepytime Dr.

GPS Coordinates: 40.0614° N, -105.2176° W

Did You Know? The first blend of Celestial Seasonings tea was brewed with chamomile, spearmint, and lemongrass harvested from Boulder's own forests.

Eldorado Canyon State Park

Need a change of perspective? Get out of the city and into the wilds. Eldorado Canyon is the perfect day trip from Boulder. Hikers, climbers, and picnickers alike can all have their day in the sun. Eldorado Canyon State Park is a day park only, so while there is no camping overnight, there is still plenty to see. Hit Rattlesnake Gulch Trail (3 miles round trip) to spy the spooky remains of the Crags Hotel that burnt down in 1913, or keep it short with a quick 30-minute trek on the Fowler Trail for a great view of the canyon.

The remaining trails, Walker Ranch Loop and Eldorado Canyon Trail, are both over 5 miles long round trip, but hikers can ride a bike or take it on horseback. For those who want to go vertical, Eldorado Canyon is a premier spot for rock climbing. There are over 500 technical routes, and some cliff faces are already equipped with bolted anchors.

Best Time to Visit: Snow can close access to the park from October through April.

Pass/Permit/Fees: $10 per vehicle, $4 per individual

Closest City or Town: Boulder

How to Get There: From Boulder, take CO-93 S/Broadway for 5.1 miles. Turn right onto Eldorado Springs Dr., and the park is in 3.1 miles at 9 Kneale Rd.

GPS Coordinates: 39.9290° N, -105.2941° W

Did You Know? The rocks at the entrance of the park are over 1.5 billion years old.

Estes Park

Estes Park is the home base of Rocky Mountain National Park. Hike or drive the Trail Ridge Road, or explore the nearby Roosevelt National Forest. The Aerial Tramway takes you to the top of Prospect Mountain for an amazing aerial view of the city. Elk can be seen in town foraging year round, and the city itself is open all year, with camping, kayaking, hiking, and water sports available in fall and summer. The tram is also open from May to September. The winter months can be an excellent time to visit to avoid the crowds that fill the city during the spring and summer. Snow blankets the area, and the views are intimate and immaculate. Cold weather sports include snowshoeing, ice climbing, and sledding.

Best Time to Visit: Estes Park is open year round, but the weather is best during the summer months. Visitors who come during spring or brave the winter months can enjoy fewer crowds and more intimate accommodations.

Pass/Permit/Fees: None but don't forget to account for food and lodgings before traveling.

Closest City or Town: Boulder

How to Get There: From Boulder, take US-36 W. From Denver, take I-25 N and exit for US-36 W toward Boulder.

GPS Coordinates: 40.3772° N, -105.5217° W

Did You Know? The haunted Stanley Hotel in Estes Park inspired Stephen King's thriller *The Shining* after the author stayed there on vacation.

Fiske Planetarium

The Megastar Star Ball projector inside the Fiske Planetarium and Science Center is the largest of its kind. Your view of space is captured across 6 projectors and shown in 8K resolution. Fly to the moon or dive into the darkness of the Arctic Ocean. Feature films on the 360-degree screen include short features from the NASA Exploration Series; light, laser, and liquid sky shows; and full-length educational films that touch on the origins of our universe and how global warming affects our planet. Some films come with VR experiences, so plan ahead if there is a feature you want to see. Public shows are always offered on the weekends, but weekday shows are limited. The facility is only open to students, class field trips, and reserved rentals for most of the spring and summer.

Best Time to Visit: Weekends are best for matinee shows.

Pass/Permit/Fees: $10 for adults or $7 for students, teachers, and children

Closest City or Town: Boulder

How to Get There: In Boulder, head east on Arapahoe Ave., then turn right on 28th St., right again on Colorado Ave., and left on Regent Dr. From Regent Dr., take a left onto Kittredge Loop Dr. to reach the planetarium at 2414 Regent Dr.

GPS Coordinates: 40.0036° N, -105.2634° W

Did You Know? The Cosmic Origins Spectrograph, featured in one of Fiske's films, recently discovered how the Milky Way recycles hydrogen gas.

Flagstaff Mountain

Flagstaff Mountain Summit is one of the most overlooked trails in Boulder, which is a shame because the overlook of the Continental Divide at the top is one of the best views in the state. It may not be the highest peak in Colorado, but at almost 7,000 feet up, you'll still feel like you're on top of the world. There is a paved road to the summit if you don't want to hike, but there's little excitement there. Instead, hit the trail at the Gregory Canyon Trailhead to catch sight of wild turkeys and bobcats. There are tiny pockets of peace away from the road and even a climbing area at Crown Rock Trail. The hike to the top of Flagstaff Mountain is 6 miles round trip with a 1,120-foot gain in elevation, so come prepared. The climb itself is moderate, but areas may not be clearly marked. Take your time and follow signs for Summit Road and the Ute and Rangeview Trails.

Best Time to Visit: September, October, November

Pass/Permit/Fees: $5 per daily parking pass

Closest City or Town: Boulder

How to Get There: In Boulder, head west on Arapahoe Ave., then left on 9th St. Turn right on Baseline Rd., and continue to Flagstaff Rd. to reach the mountain.

GPS Coordinates: 40.0017° N, -105.3075° W

Did You Know? A tiny one-roomed cave is tucked away at the buttress of Flagstaff Mountain.

Mount Sanitas Hiking Trail

Take the Mount Sanitas Hiking Trail and you're walking on a piece of Boulder history. The Boulder-Colorado Sanitarium and Hospital built the hiking trail for its tuberculosis patients in 1902. The high altitude and thin air were believed to improve respiratory health, and the Mount Sanitas Hiking Trail can still be used today for a wellness hike. The trailhead offers up one of the most unobstructed views of all of Boulder from the summit, and there are several false summits and outcroppings along the way to rest and take in the scenery before you continue the climb to the top. The hike is an easy one, but the trails are steep. You will stop to catch your breath more than once. Hikers can choose to take the shorter Mount Sanitas Valley Hike Out-and-Back Trail or the Dakota Ridge Trail for an easier trek, but if you want the sweeping view of Boulder from above, you'll have to brave the Mount Sanitas Loop.

Best Time to Visit: April through August, and come for a morning hike when the trail is less busy

Pass/Permit/Fees: None, although you may have to pay for parking

Closest City or Town: Boulder

How to Get There: In Boulder, head north on Broadway, then turn right on Mapleton Ave. and continue to Sunshine Dr. to reach the trailhead.

GPS Coordinates: 40.0273° N, -105.3007° W

Did You Know? The Sanitas Valley Trail was originally a wagon road used by sandstone miners in the 1920s.

Pearl Street Mall

There's no predicting what you'll see as you explore the four blocks of Pearl Street Mall. Street performers and musicians entertain from the sidewalk, while aromas from nearby restaurants perfume the air, and art galleries show off pieces from across the world. If you visit during the winter, the street is overrun with twinkling lights, and in the spring, tulips bloom along the flowerbeds that line the street. Take a seat at the farm-to-table restaurants on the West End to support local businesses. There are also a few bakeries and a chocolate shop if you're already thinking about dessert. If you're on the Eastside, you'll find rows of shopping, more restaurants, and a chance to explore the history of Boulder through some of the city's oldest buildings.

Best Time to Visit: Visit the mall during the late afternoon and early evening to catch a glimpse of the performers and enjoy dinner.

Pass/Permit/Fees: It's free to visit the mall, but parking costs $1.25 per hour in the garage with some free parking available on the street.

Closest City or Town: Boulder

How to Get There: In Boulder, head north on Broadway toward Pearl St. to reach the mall at 1942 Broadway 301.

GPS Coordinates: 40.0181° N, -105.2794° W

Did You Know? The New York deli featured in the 1970s sitcom *Mork & Mindy* was once located on the 1100 block of Pearl Street.

The Flatirons

Locals don't call them mountains. The Flatirons are a rock formation framing the Green Mountain, making it one of the most iconic spots in Boulder. Flatirons 1–5 run north to south along the mountain, and there are many smaller unnumbered formations scattered about to climb and explore. Rock climbing is most popular on the First and Third Flatirons, and hikers can find trails tucked throughout the rocks. Take a leisurely 2-mile hike on the Flatiron Loop Trail, or take the rougher terrain of the 3-mile Royal Arch Trail for even more breathtaking views. Although the winter months are the best time to see the Flatirons, visiting during summer gives you a chance to smell them, too. Summer heat on the ponderosa pines cooks up aromas of chocolate and ice cream, turning the Flatirons into a treat for all five senses.

Best Time to Visit: Winter. Bring snowshoes or snow cleats to safely enjoy this winter hike.

Pass/Permit/Fees: Free to hike, $5 to park

Closest City or Town: Boulder

How to Get There: From Boulder, turn left on 9th St., then right on Baseline Rd. In 322 feet, turn left onto Kinnikinnick Rd., and you'll arrive at the Flatirons in 115 feet.

GPS Coordinates: 39.9866° N, -105.2939° W

Did You Know? Look out for a large *C-U* atop the Third Flatiron, painted there in 1949 by two Colorado University freshmen.

The Hill

From vintage bars and shopping to arts festivals and concerts, University Hill is your return to the urban in Boulder. The Hill itself offers local eats, grocers, coffee shops, and even a barber, but Event Street is your premier stop for outdoor shopping and performances, including protests, poetry readings, and live music.

University Hill is home to the students, fraternities, and sororities of the nearby University of Colorado, which lends a specific kind of vibe to the neighborhood. The Hill was home to many counterculture movements in the 1970s, and you will pick up on that energy as you explore the streets and get to know the locals.

Best Time to Visit: Early autumn when the shops in the Hill are open and classes have started

Pass/Permit/Fees: None, but you may have to pay for street or garage parking

Closest City or Town: Boulder

How to Get There: In Boulder, head east on Arapahoe toward Broadway, then turn left on 9th and left again on College Ave. to reach University Hill.

GPS Coordinates: 40.0072° N, -105.2795° W

Did You Know? Two local bars, The Sink and Tulagi's, are the originals from back when Boulder used to be a dry city and bars could only sell 3.2% beer.

Valmont Bike Park

The Valmont Bike Park was 15 years in the making. The project was originally proposed in 1996 but did not open until 2011 after private fundraising, donations, and an eventual city investment made it possible to open and remain free to the public for the foreseeable future.

Bikers of all types and skill levels will find a few new favorite trails in this 42-acre park. Grab some air on a dirt jump, or have a little fun at the pump park. There are family trails wide enough for everyone, cyclocross courses for the extreme athletes, and cross-country trails for the outdoor explorer. Don't be afraid to bring the little ones. Between the playground and the kid's trails, there's plenty of room for everyone to have fun on two legs or two wheels.

Best Time to Visit: The park is open all year round, but summer and early autumn offer the best weather for riding.

Pass/Permit/Fees: Free for individual bikers, though fees will be assessed for bigger groups, rentals, and events

Closest City or Town: Boulder

How to Get There: In Boulder, from Arapahoe Ave., turn left onto Foothills Pkwy., and then right onto Valmont Rd. to reach the park at 3160 Airport Rd.

GPS Coordinates: 40.0319° N, -105.2335° W

Did You Know? The skate park cost $3.2 million to build.

Paint Mines Interpretive Park

Paint Mines Interpretive Park showcases 4 miles of trails over 750 acres of prairies, grasslands, wetlands, and the colorful geological formations known as "the Hoodoos." The Hoodoos are tall spires of sandstone and rock formed over centuries of erosion, revealing colorful purple, red, and yellow layers underneath. Visitors can choose to drive or hike the Paint Mines Trail to the formations. Free parking is available, and historical markers along the trail note the different archaeological discoveries made there.

Best Time to Visit: Spring months are the best for hiking and nature trips.

Pass/Permit/Fees: The park is free to enter every day from dusk until dawn.

Closest City or Town: Colorado Springs

How to Get There: From Colorado Springs, turn right onto E. Platte Ave from N. Nevada Ave. Continue onto US-24 E/E. Platte Ave for 0.6 miles. Keep left to stay on US-24 E. In 28.2 miles, turn right onto Yoder St. Continue onto N. Calhan Hwy. In 0.4 miles, turn left onto Paint Mine Rd. In 1.4 miles, the destination will be on the left at 29950 Paint Mine Rd.

GPS Coordinates: 39.0207° N, -104.2744° W

Did You Know? Paint Mines Interpretive Park is an archaeological district with evidence of human life dating back more than 9,000 years.

Royal Gorge Bridge and Park

The Arkansas River slowly carved this 1,200-foot gorge into the mountains outside Cañon City. If you're brave enough, you can cross Royal Gorge via the 1,270-foot suspension bridge. Don't worry—it's only 956 feet up in the air. If that doesn't get your blood pumping, sign up for a rock-climbing adventure up the gorge with a trained mountain guide. Your bravery will be rewarded with amazing views that most tourists don't get the privilege of seeing. But you don't need to climb a mountain to be a daredevil. Take a ride on the Royal Rush Skycoaster instead, which lets you free fall and dangle over the edge of the gorge. If you'd rather relax and enjoy the view, a low-adrenaline but breathtaking ride on the Royal Gorge Route Railroad will give you a unique view from below the gorge along the Arkansas River.

Best Time to Visit: Late fall and early spring are the best times to avoid the crowds.

Pass/Permit/Fees: $23 per adult, $23 per child ages 6–12, free for children 5 and under

Closest City or Town: Cañon City

How to Get There: From Cañon City, take US-50 W/Royal Gorge Blvd. to County Rd 3A. In 4.3 miles, turn left to reach the park at 4218 County Rd 3A.

GPS Coordinates: 38.4632° N, -105.3224° W

Did You Know? Allosaurus, stegosaurus, and the brontosaurus all roamed the Royal Gorge millions of years before humans arrived.

Skyline Drive

Ever wanted to drive across a razorback mountain? Take Skyline Drive in Cañon City and hold on tight. There are no guardrails to protect your vehicle from the sheer cliff face, and the inclines can get steep at some parts. It's barely over 2.5 miles long but ends in an epic panoramic view of the Arkansas River Valley and Hogback Hills. Keep an eye out for ankylosaurus prints from the Cretaceous Period just past the entrance.

Skyline Drive is a one-way street, so you cannot turn around. Fortunately, there are plenty of pull-offs along the way where you can take a breath, rest your nerves, and get a picture of the amazing sights. To extend the adventure, get out of the car and take a quick hike up the mile-long Old Skyline Drive Trail.

Best Time to Visit: Scoot down Skyline Drive any time of year for an amazing view.

Pass/Permit/Fees: Free

Closest City or Town: Cañon City

How to Get There: From Canon City, take Franklin Ave to 15th St., and stay on 15th St. until you can take a right onto US-50 W/Royal Gorge Blvd. In 4.2 miles, turn onto Skyline Dr.

GPS Coordinates: 38.4619° N, -105.2516° W

Did You Know? Sixty inmates from Cañon City Territorial Prison built Skyline Drive and earned 10 days off their sentence for every 30 they worked.

The Winery at Holy Cross Abbey

Sip on award-winning wines and bask in the arms of the Sangre de Cristo Mountains. Every wine is handcrafted, crushed, and bottled by winemaker Jeff Stulz, who opened the winery in 2002. Originally built as a monastery in 1924, many of the buildings are still used today. The tasting room is housed in the Arts and Crafts Cottage and features foodstuffs, locally made crafts, and, of course, the Abbey's award-winning wine. Taste viogniers, cabernets, rieslings, and merlots as you feast al fresco from the menu. Dining is only offered on the weekends from October through May, but you can place orders any day of the week during the summer.

Best Time to Visit: Tours and tastings happen all year round, but it's best to come at the end of September for the Annual Harvest Festival.

Pass/Permit/Fees: $8 for a flight

Closest City or Town: Cañon City

How to Get There: From Cañon City, take US-50 E/Royal Gorge Blvd. to Fremont Dr. Take two rights to access the Winery at 3011 US-50.

GPS Coordinates: 38.4492° N, -105.1983° W

Did You Know? Holy Cross Abbey has taken many forms over the years, from a monastery to a boarding school, and now a winery.

Crystal Mill

This is one of the most photogenic spots in Colorado. The mill, which balances contentedly above a raging river, appears to be from a fairytale universe. It inspires a sense of magical serenity, so you'll want to visit early in the day to avoid the crowds. Guided tours of the mill are available, including horseback riding tours through the forest, and paths are open to hikers and bikers who wish to reach Crystal Mill on their own. For more Instagrammable moments, continue past the mill to visit the ghost town of Crystal. Crystal Mill is located on County Rd. 3 a few miles past Highway 133. Bogan Flats Campground offers RV-friendly sites along the county road, and nearby Beaver Lake is another popular spot in the summer.

Best Time to Visit: Sunrise or sunset in the spring and summer months to capture the perfect photo

Pass/Permit/Fees: Free to hike and photograph, $10 to swim

Closest City or Town: Carbondale

How to Get There: From Carbondale, take CO-133 S for 20.9 miles, and then turn left onto County Rd. 3. Turn left onto W. 1st St., right onto W. Main St., left onto E. 2nd St., and then right onto E. Silver St. to reach the mill at 11520 County Rd. 3.

GPS Coordinates: 39.0590° N, -107.1045° W

Did You Know? Crystal Mill wasn't actually a mill at all but a water turbine used to power mining equipment for nearby Crystal Mine.

Pikes Peak Summit

Pikes Peak just might be the most visited mountain in the country. At over 14,000 feet above sea level, it's among the tallest in the state, and visitors can reach it by bike, train, car, or on a good old-fashioned hike.

Barr Trail is a 26-mile round trip that takes you to Pikes Peak Summit. Stop halfway at Barr Camp to stay overnight. The hike can take up to 10 hours, so if you don't plan on doing it in one day, book a campsite early. Barr Camp is the only place to stay on the trail overnight, and sites fill up quickly. For a less intense and shorter hike, take the 4-mile Crags Trail (suitable for families) or the 6-mile Catamount Trail. However, neither leads to the summit.

Best Time to Visit: Spring and early summer are the best times for a hike when the trailheads are less crowded. Watch out for a chance rainstorm or two.

Pass/Permit/Fees: $35 per vehicle, $10 per adult, $5 per child under 15

Closest City or Town: Cascade

How to Get There: From Cascade, head north on Fountain Ave and take a left onto Pikes Peak Hwy. In 19 miles, turn right to access Barr Trailhead. There are tolls for this route.

GPS Coordinates: 38.8406° N, -105.0419° W

Did You Know? There can be a 40-degree difference in temperature between the base of Pikes Peak and the summit.

Steamboat Lake State Park

Located at the base of Hahn's Peak, Steamboat Lake State Park is another healthy balance of history and the outdoors. Take on the 5.5 miles of trails or explore the nearby historic towns of Clark and Hahn's Peak, Colorado. Tombstone Trail is the most popular hiking trail in the park. At 1.1 miles, it's an easy trail that connects the gold-mining history of the state with the Routt National Forest.

If you want to get wet, camp in the state park over the summer to get the most out of the marina and the lake that is its namesake. The marina is still in operation, and visitors can rent steamboats, kayaks, paddleboards, or motorboats. Visitors can still enjoy the water during the winter, especially for fishing. Ice fishing, fly fishing, and pier fishing are open all year round with a license. Hunting season also begins in the winter, starting in November.

Best Time to Visit: May through November. Boating and swimming are only available from May 1–September 1.

Pass/Permit/Fees: $9 per vehicle, $4 per individual

Closest City or Town: Clark

How to Get There: From Clark, head west on County Rd. 60 toward County Rd. 129. Turn right onto Co Rd. 129, and then take another left onto Sage Flats to reach Steamboat Lake State Rd. at 61105 Rcr 129.

GPS Coordinates: 40.7972° N, -106.9660° W

Did You Know? While Steamboat Lake is at the base of the mountain, there is a watchtower at the very top.

Bishop Castle

Bishop Castle is always free to visit. Explore the grounds and soak up the audaciousness of this homage to Gothic architecture. One man's dream to build a snug little cabin in the woods for his wife has grown into a magical castle the Grimm brothers would envy.

James Bishop is always building onto his castle. The glass ceilings and arched windows point upwards to turreted towers and an angry dragon ready to pop off. The highest tower reaches nearly 160 feet, and James makes no promises that he won't try to build one higher.

Don't miss the pull-off at 12705 CO-165 (a ways past Bigelow Creek). You should see other vehicles parked along the road. A short and slightly steep walk up the driveway leads to the castle, and self-guided tours are free.

Best Time to Visit: The castle is open year round. Tour the grounds on the weekends to view construction in real time.

Pass/Permit/Fees: Free to visit

Closest City or Town: Colorado City

How to Get There: In Colorado City, take Bent Brothers Blvd. to CO-165 W, and the castle is on the left in 21.5 miles at 12705 CO-165.

GPS Coordinates: 38.0614° W, -105.0944° N

Did You Know? James Bishop, owner and builder of Bishop Castle, bought the land for $450 when he was 15 years old.

Cheyenne Mountain Zoo

Cheyenne Mountain Zoo is home to 800 animals, including 30 endangered species. Take a stroll through the exhibits before taking a ride on the zoo's historic carousel or hopping onto the Mountaineer Sky Ride. The sky-high ski lift drifts through grizzly bear and mountain goat exhibits built right into the Rockies. Feed the giraffes, hang out with a sloth, meet the big cats, or create art with a porcupine at this zoo! Private guided tours are available in addition to seasonal activities and opportunities.

Best Time to Visit: Avoid the summer crowds and visit during the winter.

Pass/Permit/Fees: Adults are $19.75/$24.75 and children are $14.75/$19.75 for weekday/weekend passes.

Closest City or Town: Colorado Springs

How to Get There: From Colorado Springs, head south and take a right onto Pikes Peak Ave. At the next cross street, turn left onto S. Nevada Ave. Continue straight to stay on S. Nevada Ave. Get onto S. Tejon St., and at the traffic circle, take the first exit onto Cheyenne Blvd. Turn left onto Cresta Rd, which becomes Mesa Ave. In 0.2 miles, continue onto Park Avenue. Continue onto Park Ave and then El Pomar Rd. Turn left onto Penrose Blvd. Continue onto Cheyenne Mountain Zoo Rd., which will bring you to the zoo at 4250 Cheyenne Mountain Zoo Rd.

GPS Coordinates: 38.7705° N, -104.8520° W

Did You Know? Cheyenne Mountain Zoo is the highest zoo in America at 6,800 feet above sea level.

Garden of the Gods

The beautiful views at the Garden of the Gods were created millions of years ago. Glacial erosion during the Ice Age contributed to most of the formations you'll see today. Stop at the visitor center before venturing out on any of the 15 miles of trails to learn more about the red rocks or the history of the Garden of the Gods, get maps, or sign up for a guided tour. Start on the Perkins Central Garden Trail, a 1.5-mile paved path, or take the easy 1-mile hike on the Siamese Twins Trail to spy a peek of Pike's Peak, the 14,115-foot-high behemoth. Rock climbing, horseback riding, biking, Segways, and Jeeps are all allowed on guided tours.

Best Time to Visit: The best time to visit the park is sunset or sunrise, September through April.

Pass/Permit/Fees: The Garden of the Gods is free to the public from 5 a.m. to 10 p.m.

Closest City or Town: Colorado Springs

How to Get There: From Colorado Springs, take E. Colorado Ave and turn left onto 14th St. Merge onto US-24 W, and in 1.7 miles, take a slight right onto S. 31st St. Turn right onto Westmoor Dr. Turn left onto N. 30th St. Garden of the Gods Visitor Center will be on the right at 1805 N. 30th St.

GPS Coordinates: 38.87.84° N, -104.8698° W

Did You Know? The Garden of the Gods got its name when a surveyor declared the spot to be the perfect place for a beer garden. His companion disagreed.

Glen Eyrie Castle

William Jackson Palmer, the founder of Colorado Springs, built Glen Eyrie Castle for himself and his wife. It was their dream home. It consists of 24 fireplaces and over 30 rooms, including 2 dining rooms, a library, and a 2,200-square-foot great hall that holds up to 240 people. Glen Eyrie is host to many weddings and formal events throughout the year, and public tours are offered twice a day during the week and three times over the weekend. Stop by for afternoon tea every Wednesday and Sunday, and enjoy handcrafted treats with the Garden of the Gods in the background. Hiking trails around the castle are open to the public unless otherwise posted. Wildfires may affect your hiking plans, so check with the castle staff or park rangers before hitting the trail.

Best Time to Visit: With no air conditioning in the castle, it's best to visit in autumn.

Pass/Permit/Fees: Tours are $9 per person and free for children under 5.

Closest City or Town: Colorado Springs

How to Get There: In Colorado Springs, from N. Nevada Ave., turn left on Uintah St. and right on Mesa Rd., then keep left on 30th St. to reach the castle at 3820 N. 30th St.

GPS Coordinates: 38.8918° N, -104.8857° W

Did You Know? Overnight stays at Glen Eyrie can include a scavenger hunt, hiking trips, and a writer's retreat.

Manitou Incline Trail

The Manitou Incline Trail is considered one of the most intense hikes in Colorado. It's just over a mile long but gains some 2,000 feet of elevation with inclines as steep as 68 percent in some areas. The 2,744 steps of Manitou Incline were initially a railroad track for the hydroelectric plant at the top. When a rockslide destroyed the track in 1990, the railroad tracks were removed, leaving behind the ties as steps. There are many bailout points along this intense trail. The false summit is about three quarters of the way up the incline (about 300 steps from the top), giving hikers a fantastic view as well as an exit point through Barr Trail.

Best Time to Visit: Spring and fall are the best seasons to climb the incline.

Pass/Permit/Fees: The incline is free to the public, but you may have to pay for parking.

Closest City or Town: Colorado Springs

How to Get There: From Colorado Springs, take US-24 W, then turn left on Serpentine Dr. At the traffic circle, take the second exit onto Manitou Ave. At the next traffic circle, take the first exit onto Ruxton Ave. Ruxton Ave. turns slightly right and becomes Winter St. Continue onto Ruxton Ave. for 0.1 miles, then take a right onto Hydro St. to reach the Manitou Incline Trail.

GPS Coordinates: 38.8576° N, -104.9128° W

Did You Know? The fastest climb to the top of the incline was clocked at 17 minutes and 45 seconds by Joseph Gray.

Mesa Verde National Park

The views from inside Mesa Verde National Park span across four states (Colorado, Arizona, Utah, and New Mexico), so take it all in. This park is one of the oldest and most extensive preservations of the Ancestral Puebloan civilization. The Puebloans built their homes into the cliffs more than 700 years ago, and many tours are only accessible by rope ladders and tunnels. The 700 Years Tour specifically takes hikers through a chronological journey of the Ancestral Puebloan lands, starting with the earliest recorded village and including a walking tour through the Cliff Palace. Take guided tours through the Cliff Palace and Balcony House, or take a hike on your own to the Long House or the Spruce Tree House. Private tours are also available. Visitors should sign up early.

Best Time to Visit: Since the park is packed in the summer and dwellings are closed for winter, spring and fall are best.

Pass/Permit/Fees: Weekly passes are available for $20–$30. Annual passes cost $55.

Closest City or Town: Cortez

How to Get There: From Cortez, head east on US-160 E toward Market St. Take the exit toward Mesa Verde National Park. Turn right onto Mesa Top Ruins Rd. You'll enter the park in 256 feet.

GPS Coordinates: 37.2309° N, -108.4618° W

Did You Know? Wildfires uncovered 593 previously unknown archaeological sites after surging through the park in 1996 and 2000.

Mollie Kathleen Gold Mine

Mollie Kathleen Gortner was one of the first women to make claim to gold in Cripple Creek. Although she died only a short 25 years later, her son managed and maintained the family mine until his death in 1949. Today, the gold mine remains open for tourists to explore.

Exploring Mollie Kathleen Gold Mine means dropping 1,000 feet below ground in a tiny elevator. You will see how gold was extracted in the 19th century and learn why Cripple Creek called itself "The World's Greatest Gold Camp."

It is the only gold mine tour in Colorado that gets this up close with the state's mining history, and tourists have been asking to see it since the turn of the century. It does get chilly below ground, so bring a jacket.

Best Time to Visit: Tours are only available from May through October.

Pass/Permit/Fees: $25 for adults, $15 for children

Closest City or Town: Colorado Springs

How to Get There: From Colorado Springs, take US-24 W to CO-67 S. The gold mine is in 16.9 miles at 9388 CO-67.

GPS Coordinates: 38.7536° N, -105.1605° W

Did You Know? The original mine tours were done by candlelight by miners who would take turns helping visitors ride down in an open ore bucket.

National Museum of World War II Aviation

With 28 fully restored military aircraft and over 4,000 artifacts, history buffs can easily get lost here. Visitors are welcome to explore the museum on their own or sign up for guided tours that go deeper into the technology used to develop flying military aircraft. Guided tours are also available for the Westpac restoration facility, where you can get a closer look at what goes into keeping these planes in mint condition. Throughout the year, the museum plans special events, photo days, air shows, and school programs. Check the museum's calendar before you go to make sure you don't miss out on anything.

Best Time to Visit: Weekends are the best time to visit.

Pass/Permit/Fees: $15 per adult, $13 for seniors and military, $11 for children. Free for WWII veterans and children under 4. Guided tours are an additional $5.

Closest City or Town: Colorado Springs

How to Get There: In Colorado Springs, take E. Platte Ave. to CO-21 S/US-24 W/N. Powers Blvd. toward S. Powers Blvd. Turn left onto Aeroplaza Dr., left onto Newport Rd., and left onto Aviation Way. The museum is on the right at 775 Aviation Way.

GPS Coordinates: 38.8214° N, -104.7202° W

Did You Know? As a reconnaissance fighter, the P-38 Lightning is responsible for nearly 90% of all aerial footage of WWII Europe.

Rainbow Falls

Hop on the Rainbow Falls Trailhead right from the parking lot in the recreation area and follow the short trail (barely 0.2 miles round trip) to the waterfalls. Locals call it "Graffiti Falls," and the street art on the canyon wall lends a colorful vibe. But it won't last long.

After floods in 2013 wrecked much of the trailhead, local citizens came together to restore the path and the bridge under the falls. Since 2016, the state has been making repairs. The graffiti will be removed, and efforts are underway to keep graffiti off the falls in the future.

Rainbow Falls is a day trip only. Overnight stays are not allowed and neither is swimming. Due to erosion and litter, the water is not safe for wading, swimming, or pets.

Best Time to Visit: The falls are open all year round, but the snow runoff in late spring makes the falls something spectacular.

Pass/Permit/Fees: $1 donation

Closest City or Town: Colorado Springs

How to Get There: From Colorado Springs, travel on US-24 W for 4.6 miles, and take a left onto Serpentine Dr. The falls will be on the right.

GPS Coordinates: 38.8681° N, -104.9243° W

Did You Know? The entrance to Rainbow Falls is across from the Cave of Winds, a famous spot near the Manitou Cliff Dwellings.

Rock Ledge Ranch Historic Site

Rock Ledge Ranch is a living museum and working farm. Tour through two centuries of Colorado history with period-appropriate museum guides leading you through the Ute tribe's Camp Creek Valley, the homesteaders' cabins, and the early settlers' farmhouse and estate.

Each historical household provides a unique point of view into the lifestyle of these different peoples, from cooking to farming. The blacksmith shop on site shows smiths and their apprentices at work repairing commercial and mining tools, and annual events invite visitors to participate in different living history programs. During the summer, Rock Ledge Ranch hosts tea luncheons that include finger sandwiches and snacks, hot tea, and a tour of all the historic sites on the ranch.

Best Time to Visit: August through October

Pass/Permit/Fees: $8 for adults, $5 for seniors, $4 for children, and $6 for military with ID

Closest City or Town: Colorado Springs

How to Get There: In Colorado Springs, head east on Colorado Ave., then turn right on 22nd St. and left on Uintah St. Turn right again on 30th St., then left onto Gateway Rd. to reach the ranch at 3105 Gateway Rd.

GPS Coordinates: 38.8774° N, -104.8714° W

Did You Know? If you want to learn how to blacksmith, visit in March to attend Rock Ledge Ranch's annual blacksmith workshop.

Trail 401

Trail 401 in Crested Butte was designed with mountain bikers in mind. Steep grades and technical pathways make it a trail for the advanced rider, but it's worth the burn to take in the epic view of the Gothic Road and the Elk Mountain Range.

Hit the trail in early spring, and the path will be lined with knee-high wildflowers that complement the peaks. On your way down, you'll have two options to get back. One course is shorter and travels down the 401, while the other is steeper but rewards you with stunning views from the upper parts of the trail. If you're planning a summer bike ride, be aware that the paths get dusty due to dry weather and increased crowds. Wear a mask to protect yourself.

Best Time to Visit: April through October. The trail is closed during the winter, so come in the spring to hike in the wildflowers.

Pass/Permit/Fees: None

Closest City or Town: Crested Butte

How to Get There: From Crested Butte, head west on Elk Ave., then turn left onto 1st St. Turn left onto Whiterock Ave., then right onto CO-135 S. Turn left onto Brush Creek Rd., then take another left onto Skyland Dr.

GPS Coordinates: 38.9010° N, -106.9672° W

Did You Know? Crested Butte is the wildflower capital of the world.

16th Street Mall

If you want to see Denver come to life, head to 16th Street and take a stroll along the quarter-mile loop. Street performers, offbeat cafes, and hundreds of local shops lay ahead.

A free shuttle service stops at every intersection, picking visitors up at Union Station to the Civic Center and back again. The bus also connects with the rail network, making it possible to visit 16th Street no matter where you're staying in Denver.

Day and night are two different experiences, and you'll likely stop along this block more than once just to see what's happening. Locals host seasonal festivals all year long, and people watching peaks in the early summer months, but there's always something going on at the mall. Don't let the cold weather stop you.

Best Time to Visit: May through October

Pass/Permit/Fees: None, although you may have to pay for parking

Closest City or Town: Denver

How to Get There: In Denver, from 15th St., turn right onto Welton St., left onto 18th St., and then take another left onto Arapahoe St. to reach the mall at 1001 16th St.

GPS Coordinates: 39.7478° N, -104.9949° W

Did You Know? The sidewalks on the mall are designed to look like the western diamondback rattlesnake.

Coors Field

Coors Field and Dodger Stadium are the only two sports fields built specifically for baseball in the country, and the Colorado Rockies have been playing home games here since 1995. If you catch a game, bring a mitt. More home runs are hit here than in any other park, thanks to the mile-high altitude. The thinner air helps baseballs fly faster and farther, and the outfield fences are farther away from home plate to accommodate the big hitters. No matter where you sit, the view is spectacular—from the game to the Rocky Mountains. The stadium holds nearly 51,000 fans, and there is a Coors microbrewery right inside, with another craft bar boasting 52 beers on tap. On top of that, the high-tech stadium boasts solar panels, a vintage clock tower, and fountains right in the middle of center field that splash every time the Rockies score a run.

Best Time to Visit: April through October

Pass/Permit/Fees: Rockies single-game tickets range from $7 for the rockpile to over $100 for club seats.

Closest City or Town: Denver

How to Get There: In Denver, head north on Lincoln St., then take a left onto 20th Ave. Take a right onto Market St., left on 21st St., and then another left onto Blake St. to reach Coors Field at 2001 Blake St.

GPS Coordinates: 39.7559° N, -104.9942° W

Did You Know? Baseballs used at Coors Field are stored in special humidors to help offset the effects of the high elevation.

Denver Art Museum

Since its founding in 1893, the Denver Art Museum continues to provide an impressive and immersive experience of culture, art, and history. The experience starts before you walk in. Both the Martin Building and the Frederic C. Hamilton Building are testaments to the intricate relationship between art and architecture. The Martin Building houses the museum's entire collection conveniently under one roof, while the Hamilton Building connects the Sie Welcome Center to the rest of the campus. Inside, visitors can view rotating exhibits that explore ancient American sculptures, 19th-century European art, and contemporary South African painters. If there are particular exhibits you want to see, check the Denver Art Museum calendar for an exhibition schedule.

Best Time to Visit: Summer and fall when the museum is offering its annual free days

Pass/Permit/Fees: $13 for adults; $10 for students, seniors, and military with ID; free for children. Denver residents get discounts on entrance fees.

Closest City or Town: Denver

How to Get There: In Denver, head south on Broadway, then turn right on 13th Ave., right onto Bannock St., and right again on 14th Ave.

GPS Coordinates: 39.7372° N, -104.9893° W

Did You Know? The distinctly designed Hamilton Building earned the 2007 AISC award for excellence in steel design and engineering.

Denver Botanic Gardens

This oasis in the middle of downtown Denver is home to the most extensive collection of flora in North America. There are seven different gardens to explore in the three different sections of the garden.

The formal garden entrance is in the heart of downtown, while the access point at Chatfield State Park offers up a natural meadow and historic farm. The wildflower garden is on your way to Mt. Evans, where you can walk among the beautiful blooms in the spring.

Families can't miss the Mordecai Children's Garden, where they host to year-round events, including free days, festivals, plant shows, and more. Before you plan your trip, check out the Denver Botanic Gardens calendar for special events.

Best Time to Visit: The best time to visit is in spring when the flowers are in full bloom.

Pass/Permit/Fees: $15 per adult, $11.50 for military and seniors, $11 for children and students

Closest City or Town: Denver

How to Get There: In Denver, take E. 14th Ave. to York St., and the gardens are on the right at 1007 York St.

GPS Coordinates: 39.7321° N, -104.9601° W

Did You Know? Denver Botanic Gardens is studying micropropagation, the method of growing new plants from small pieces of plant tissue.

Denver Museum of Nature & Science

The Denver Museum of Nature & Science grew from one local man's collection of flora and fauna. Edwin Carter, a biologist with a passion for Rocky Mountain wildlife, offered to sell his collection to the capital city in 1892 so that everyone could see and learn from his findings. The museum continued to excavate and explore the nearby area. It was jettisoned to the forefront of archeological research in the 1920s after 10,000-year-old human artifacts were found. Today, visitors can see those artifacts and more across the 716,000-square-foot museum. Special exhibitions change throughout the year and may cost a little extra, but you can't always put a price on unique experiences like getting lost in a mirror maze or flying with birds.

Best Time to Visit: The museum is open all year round but offers free days throughout the year, from January to early December.

Pass/Permit/Fees: $20 per adult, $15 per child, $17 per senior with an extra $5 for the planetarium, $7 for IMAX, and $9 for special exhibits

Closest City or Town: Denver

How to Get There: In Denver, head east on 17th Ave., then turn left on High St., then right on 23rd Ave.

GPS Coordinates: 39.7475° N, -104.9428° W

Did You Know? A collection and restoration center housing more than 4 million artifacts is hard at work two stories below the museum.

Denver Skate Park at LoDo

This Denver skate park is the largest free park of its kind in the country, and skaters of all skill levels are invited to shred 7 days a week. There are the traditional bowls and half-pipes every skater knows, but there are also a few unique street skating features you might not be expecting scattered across the park's 60,000 square feet. During its construction, the skate park at LoDo (Lower Downtown) began as a humble street course with a few bowls, including a kidney-shaped number. The second phase expanded it to include more street features, and the final 10,000 square feet were built into a snake run in 2002. You don't have to skate to enjoy the park. Bikers and rollerbladers are always welcome, and spectators even have their own section. A promenade around the park gives those without wheels a chance to explore and take in the views of downtown Denver.

Best Time to Visit: The skate park is open seven days a week.

Pass/Permit/Fees: None. It's free to skate.

Closest City or Town: Denver

How to Get There: In Denver, head north on Lincoln St. and turn left on 20th St. Take another left onto Little Raven St., then a right onto 19th St. to reach 2205 19th St.

GPS Coordinates: 39.7596° N, -105.0028° W

Did You Know? Denver Parks & Recreation invested $1.5 million in the skate park to prevent youth from being ticketed for skateboarding at the 16th Street Mall.

Denver Zoo

The Denver Zoo is worth a visit for every animal lover. From meet-and-greet animal experiences to cultural performances, there is more to the wildlife here than meets the eye. Families are always welcome, but adults can enjoy special child-free events and tours of the zoo on select days. Visitors can get to know their scaly neighbors in the serpentarium and take a tour of the jungle with the latest Tropical Discovery exhibit, which gets up-close-and-personal with sloths, tree frogs, Komodo dragons, and a Siamese crocodile named Daphne. Spending the whole day at the zoo also means catching one or more of the many demonstrations that go on almost daily. Learn about capuchin monkeys, grizzly bears, and sea lions, or wait around to see who shows up at the next Wildlife Encounter at Wildlife Plaza.

Best Time to Visit: Spring, when the animals are active but the crowds are minimal

Pass/Permit/Fees: $20 for adults and seniors, $14 per child

Closest City or Town: Denver

How to Get There: In Denver, from E. 17th Ave., turn left onto Josephine St., and then right onto E. 23rd Ave. to reach the zoo at 2300 Steele St.

GPS Coordinates: 39.7502° N, -104.9490° W

Did You Know? The Denver Zoo began in 1896 with the donation of a single American black bear cub from then-mayor Thomas S. McMurry.

Elitch Gardens Theme and Water Park

There's more to Elitch Gardens than roller coasters and water slides, although the park boasts more than 50 of those. But depending on which day you visit, you can catch a drive-in movie, fireworks show, or join a holiday-themed party after screaming your guts out on the Mind Eraser.

Elitch Gardens was always more than an amusement park. From its opening day in 1890, Elitch hosted animals, symphonies, botanical gardens, and dance halls before constructing its first thrill ride in 1936. The first coaster was built in 1965, and visitors can ride an exact replica of Mister Twister today.

In 1994, the entire theme park was closed permanently and moved to its current location, and replicas of other original rides, including the original carousel and the Sidewinder and Twister II coasters, were rebuilt.

Best Time to Visit: The park is open every day in June and July and on the weekends from August through Halloween.

Pass/Permit/Fees: $69.99 per person

Closest City or Town: Denver

How to Get There: In Denver, head west on Colfax Ave., right on Speer Blvd., then left on Elitch Cir. to reach the park at 2000 Elitch Cir.

GPS Coordinates: 39.7502° N, -105.0101° W

Did You Know? Elitch was a part of Six Flags until the property was sold to the city of Denver in 2006.

Forney Museum of Transportation

Historical transportation isn't just vintage Model Ts—although those are here, too. Forney Museum boasts all sorts of vintage vehicles, including sleighs, fire trucks, buggies, and motorcycles. It even has toys and diecast model cars. The unique artifacts in the Forney Museum make it a one-of-a-kind experience. Car shows are a common scene throughout the year, and rotating exhibits examine the ways transportation shaped our country, from gold mining to baseball games.

In total, over 500 exhibits and artifacts are showcased in the museum. The slogan requires that the museum show "Anything on Wheels," and visitors will have a chance to see unique rides, such as Amelia Earhart's car and a locomotive designed by a cousin in the Forney family.

Best Time to Visit: The museum is open year round with different events and traveling exhibits. Visit in the afternoon after 2 p.m. to avoid the crowds.

Pass/Permit/Fees: $14 for adults, $13 for children, $12 for seniors

Closest City or Town: Denver

How to Get There: In Denver, head north on Broadway and continue onto E. Brighton Blvd. The museum is on the left at 4303 Brighton Blvd.

GPS Coordinates: 39.7780° N, -104.9707° W

Did You Know? The collection at the Forney Museum started with one car: Amelia Earhart's Kissel Gold Bug.

Four Mile Historic Park

Four Mile House is the oldest standing structure in Denver. It sits on 12 acres of history. Visitors are welcome to tour the museum, get to know the farm animals, or even take a goat yoga class (offered Wednesdays and weekends).

Four Mile Historic Park began as a stagecoach and tavern in the 1860s for travelers headed to Fort Laramie on the Cherokee Trail, but once railroads replaced wagon travel, it became the working farm visitors can explore today.

When the property was purchased by the city in 1975, archaeological digs happened almost immediately, revealing the foundations of many more 19th-century buildings. The museum remains open all year round to preserve the property and welcome visitors.

Best Time to Visit: June through December

Pass/Permit/Fees: $5 for adults, $4 for seniors and military veterans, $3 for children

Closest City or Town: Denver

How to Get There: In Denver, head south on Broadway and turn left on 6th Ave. Make a right onto Colorado Blvd., then turn left on Cherry Creek to reach the park at 715 S. Forest St.

GPS Coordinates: 39.7035° N, -104.9292° W

Did You Know? At its largest, Four Mile Historic Park spanned a total of 600 acres.

History Colorado Center

Learn everything you could possibly want about the state and western territory of Colorado. The History Colorado Center is dedicated to preserving the unique history of the state, and interactive exhibits give visitors a chance to travel back in time to every era of Colorado's history and founding. Other permanent exhibits showcase the Ancestral Puebloans, 19th-century homesteaders, modern residents, and how all generations are impacting the social and natural environment of Colorado. Exhibits will sometimes travel, and the center hosts all kinds of events around Denver. Various museums throughout Colorado are associated with the History Colorado Center. They're worth a visit if you're in the area, including the Fort Garland Museum and Cultural Center, the Ute Indian Museum, and the Healy House Museum.

Best Time to Visit: Mornings (museum opens at 10 a.m.)

Pass/Permit/Fees: $14 for adults, $12 for seniors, $10 for students, $8 for children

Closest City or Town: Denver

How to Get There: In Denver, take Cleveland Pl. to 16th St. Mall to reach N. Broadway. The center is at 1200 N. Broadway.

GPS Coordinates: 39.7358° N, -104.9871° W

Did You Know? The History Colorado Center stands only one block away from where the old Colorado History Museum used to be.

Molly Brown House Museum

The Unsinkable Molly Brown would not gain her worldwide fame until the sinking of the Titanic, but she was already well known in Colorado by then. Molly Brown's husband J.J. struck gold in Colorado in 1893, and the couple purchased this home on Pennsylvania Street the following year. Ironically, Molly Brown and J.J. spent most of their time traveling the world. The home was rented out by many wealthy citizens and used as the Governor's Mansion until 1926 when Molly turned it into a boarding house. Today, the home is preserved to represent the original Queen Anne architectural style. As most 19th-century homes do, the Molly Brown House Museum has narrow hallways, stairwells, and rooms. All tours are guided and can fill up quickly. Reservations are only required for large groups.

Best Time to Visit: Thursdays and Fridays are less crowded.

Pass/Permit/Fees: $14 for adults, $12 for seniors, $10 for children, $12 for students and military with ID

Closest City or Town: Denver

How to Get There: In Denver, from Cleveland Pl., turn right onto N. Broadway. Take a left onto E. 14th Ave. and a right onto Pennsylvania St. to reach the museum at 1340 Pennsylvania St.

GPS Coordinates: 39.7375° N, -104.9808° W

Did You Know? Molly and J.J. Brown originally bought the home for $30,000.

State Capitol Building

The Denver State Capitol Building is the only building in the world constructed of a rare form of rose marble that was discovered in Beulah. Colorado Rose Onyx, also known as Beulah red marble, has not been discovered elsewhere, which makes a visit to this historical building a must.

Beyond its exterior construction, the interior is home to the state Senate, Treasury, House of Representatives, and the offices of the governor and lieutenant governor. Historical tours take curious visitors into the chambers while they are in session and into the historical gilded dome. The dome itself is plated in over 12 lbs. of 24-karat gold in honor of the miners and pioneers who built Colorado and made it into the state it is today.

Best Time to Visit: Summer. Tours fill up quickly from January to May.

Pass/Permit/Fees: Guided tours are free and available Monday through Friday.

Closest City or Town: Denver

How to Get There: In Denver, from N. Broadway, turn left onto E. Colfax Ave., then take a right onto Grant St. to reach the State Building at 200 E. Colfax Ave.

GPS Coordinates: 39.7393° N, -104.9848° W

Did You Know? Along with locally sourced rose onyx, the exterior of the capitol is made with granite quarried near Gunnison.

Washington Park

The neighborhood of Washington Park is a mix of historic, urban, and outdoor adventure. Rent a kayak from the boathouse on Smith Lake, or hit one of the many trails to get a new look at downtown Denver. Visitors can stroll through the flower gardens and smell the tulips in spring, or head down to South Pearl Street for wine tasting and cocktails in autumn. There's even a Denver Beer Trail nearby for the hopheads in your travel party.

It's the perfect place for a run or bike ride, and the playground makes it an excellent stop for family picnics. No matter when you visit, Washington Park will have an adventure waiting.

Best Time to Visit: Visit in summer and early autumn to enjoy all of the outdoor activities at the park.

Pass/Permit/Fees: Washington Park is free to visit, but you may have to pay for parking.

Closest City or Town: Denver

How to Get There: In Denver, use N. Broadway to get onto 6th Ave., and then turn right onto Speer Blvd. From Speer Blvd., take N. Downing St. to E. Alameda Ave., and then turn right at E. Mississippi Ave. to reach the park.

GPS Coordinates: 39.0072° N, -104.9640° W

Did You Know? The flower garden at Lake Windemere is an exact replica of Martha Washington's garden at Mt. Vernon.

Wings Over the Rockies Air & Space Museum

Take to the skies in your choice of air or spacecraft, both literally and figuratively. There may be plenty to see on the ground, but the museum's Exploration of Flight program hosts air shows, flight school, and will take visitors up in the air with FAA-certified pilots. Aircraft exhibits showcase vintage warplanes, including the Air Force B-52 Stratofortress, Douglass B-18 Bolo, and F-104 Starfighter. Visitors will also get a modern treat with a closer look at the Star Wars X-Wing Starfighter and the Dream Chaser ISS space shuttle. If you aren't quite ready to earn your wings yet, stay grounded in the VR lounge or travel vicariously through the stories of local Colorado astronauts.

Best Time to Visit: Mornings (museum opens at 10 a.m.)

Pass/Permit/Fees: $17 for adults; $13 for seniors, military, and first responders; $10 for children

Closest City or Town: Denver

How to Get There: In Denver, head south on Broadway, then turn left on 6th Ave. and right on Syracuse St. Take a left onto E. 4th Ave. to reach the museum at 7711 E. Academy Blvd.

GPS Coordinates: 39.7201° N, -104.8958° W

Did You Know? Wings Over the Rockies is built in the historic Lowry Airforce Base.

Union Station

Union Station in Denver is both a working rail station and one of the most popular tourist destinations in the city. From a historical perspective, visitors can tour the station and the nearby Crawford Hotel before stepping back into the modern world with the Union Station Farmers Market. The original station was built in 1881 and subsequently demolished and rebuilt in 1914 with the Renaissance Revival style we see today. In 2001, Union Station was revitalized by the city as a historic building, cultural hub, and central transportation station before reopening its doors in 2014. Even if you don't have a train to catch, there's plenty to see, eat, and drink, with a bar in the historical ticketing office and an ice cream parlor in the former barbershop.

Best Time to Visit: Visit Union Station any time of year.

Pass/Permit/Fees: None, although you may have to pay for street or garage parking

Closest City or Town: Denver

How to Get There: In Denver, from 15th St., turn right onto Wynkoop St., then take another right onto Little Raven St. Take a final right onto Basset St. Union Station is on the right at 1700 Wewatta St.

GPS Coordinates: 39.7527° N, -105.0017° W

Did You Know? Denver's Union Station earned LEED certification in 2014 for its introduction of green cleaning policies and use of recycled materials.

United States Mint

The U.S. Mint has been attracting visitors since minting its first coin in Denver in 1906. Today, the facility mints numismatic and circulating-quality coins while offering free tours to every visitor over the age of 7. Before it was federally owned, the mint was founded by three brokers who were tired of paying the shipping costs to send gold back east. Establishing their own private mint removed the middleman, and the brokers were printing 15–20 coins every minute, ultimately minting over half a million dollars in gold coins before the federal government purchased the mint in 1863. If you plan on visiting the mint, leave your backpacks at home. Visitors are only allowed small wallets, umbrellas, wheelchairs/walkers, and empty water bottles.

Best Time to Visit: Summer vacation—from Memorial Day to Labor Day—is the most popular time at the mint. Visit in spring or fall to avoid the crowds.

Pass/Permit/Fees: Free, but tickets are first come, first served and sell out quickly

Closest City or Town: Denver

How to Get There: In Denver, head west on Colfax Ave. and turn left onto Cherokee St. The mint is on the right at 1450 Cherokee St.

GPS Coordinates: 39.7395° N, -104.9928° W

Did You Know? Ironically, bullion coins made with gold, silver, or platinum are minted at every facility except the one in Denver.

Dillon Reservoir

Dillon Marina at the reservoir is the highest deep-water marina in North America. It's where you can rent a pontoon boat or paddleboard in the summer and an iceboat in the winter. But the water isn't all there is at Dillon. With more than 7 miles of paved hiking trails and 350 campsites, Dillon Reservoir will inspire the outdoorsman in everyone. Take the Sapphire Point Trail to the scenic overlook of the Gore, Ten Mile, and Williams Fork mountains, then pitch a tent (or drive up your RV) by the water. Since most of the action at Dillon Reservoir happens on the water, summer is the busiest time of year. If water sports are not on your list, visit Dillon in the winter to avoid the crowds. Check out the Ice Castles, a frozen attraction of thousands of icicles hand-placed by professional artists.

Best Time to Visit: Spring months are best for avoiding the crowds.

Pass/Permit/Fees: A fishing license is required for anyone over 16.

Closest City or Town: Dillon

How to Get There: From Dillon, head south on La Bonte St. toward Buffalo St. At the traffic circle, take the second exit onto Dillon Dam Rd. to reach the reservoir.

GPS Coordinates: 39.0692° N, -106.0611° W

Did You Know? Dillon is named after Tom Dillon, a gold prospector who disappeared and turned up dead in Golden, CO.

Dinosaur National Monument

Walk with dinosaurs and get up close and personal with the Utah state border at Dinosaur National Monument. Slip over into Utah to see dinosaur fossils embedded in rock, or stay within Colorado to take a scenic drive or an off-trail hike through the Uinta Mountains. Harpers Corner Trail takes hikers 3 miles round trip on a moderate trek through the cliffs and backcountry. Off-trail hiking is allowed at the monument, and it's one of the best ways to get a closer look at the dinosaur bones and ancient petroglyphs.

Best Time to Visit: Peak season is May through September, so come earlier to beat the crowds.

Pass/Permit/Fees: $25 per vehicle (up to 14 people), $15 per individual

Closest City or Town: Dinosaur

How to Get There: From Dinosaur, head south on School St. toward 4th St. Next, School St. turns left and becomes 4th St. In 0.2 miles, turn left onto Stegosaurus Fwy., and in 0.3 miles, turn right onto US-40 E/Brontosaurus Blvd. Follow US-40 E for 1.9 miles, and then turn left onto Harpers Corner Rd. to reach the monument at 11625 E. 1500 S.

GPS Coordinates: 40.4927° N, -108.9416° W

Did You Know? The Fremont people responsible for the petroglyphs on the cliff faces lived in the area in the 14th century.

100 Mile Overlook at 105 West Ranch

An overnight stay at 105 West Ranch really provides 100 miles of beautifully breathtaking views. Pike's Peak bears down on you from the north while Beaver Creek Canyon beckons you from the south. A trailhead at the Skaguay dam leads hikers right into the canyon, or you can choose to stake out a spot and fish at Skaguay reservoir. No matter what your plan is, don't worry about packing your equipment. The Adventure Gear Shed at 105 West provides campers with SUPs, fishing rods, mountain bikes, tents, outdoor games, and chairs. Campsites can sit almost 10,000 feet above sea level and are supplied with heaters, fire pits, grills, canvas tents, and pop-up tents to keep campers comfortable. All sites at 105 are fairly remote, and safety guidelines regarding bear-proof food containers, fire safety, and Leave No Trace must be followed at all times.

Best Time to Visit: May through October to take full advantage of West Ranch's 48 acres

Pass/Permit/Fees: Private campsites start at $100 per night.

Closest City or Town: Divide

How to Get There: From Divide, take CO-67 S for 13.4 miles, and turn left onto County Rd. 81/Lazy S. Ranch Rd. Turn left onto Phantom Canyon Rd. and then right onto County Rd. 863 to reach the ranch.

GPS Coordinates: 38.6796° N, -105.0632° W

Did You Know? The family that owns 105 West Ranch has lived in Colorado since the 19th century.

Colorado Wolf and Wildlife Center

The Colorado Wolf and Wildlife Center is the one place in Colorado you can go to meet a wolf. Visitors can take feeding tours or sign up for wolf meet and greets (complete with photo op). Learn about the wolves' habitats, the ecological threats they face, and ways to help, including volunteer opportunities. Tours through the entire sanctuary take about an hour and end with a group howl that will hopefully inspire the whole pack to join in. Reservations are required, including for full-moon tours and special events. Be aware that peak season is May through September, so plan ahead if you want to meet a wolf.

Best Time to Visit: March through June is the best time to visit, but the center is open all year round. Arrive early to avoid crowds.

Pass/Permit/Fees: Standard tours cost $20 per adult and $15 per child. Meet and greets cost $120–$140 per person. VIP encounters cost $375–$450 for two people.

Closest City or Town: Divide

How to Get There: From Divide, head south on N Rd./N. Manchester Creek Rd. toward Weaver Rd. Turn right onto US-24 W. In 1.6 miles, turn left onto Twin Rocks Rd., and the center will be on the right at 4729 Twin Rocks Rd.

GPS Coordinates: 38.9306° N, -105.2120° W

Did You Know? The center began as the Wolf Hybrid Rescue Center to protect wolfdogs and educate the public about their existence.

Durango and Silverton Narrow Gauge Railroad

The railway itself is a federally designated historical landmark, and steam locomotives still carry tourists and history buffs through the Rocky Mountains with many of the same vintage comforts. Originally, the railroad carried miners, valuable gold and silver ore, and other freight back and forth between the mining towns of Durango and Silverton in the early 1880s, but it wasn't until after WWII that the train reached its stride. Today, riders are taken on a romantic ride through the San Juan National Forest and along the Animas River to enjoy a naturally majestic view that hasn't changed in over a century. Hikers can also choose to hop on the Silverton Diesel Train instead for a special chance to explore the Weminuche Wilderness Area.

Best Time to Visit: Train rides and tours vary year round.

Pass/Permit/Fees: Tickets start at $99.

Closest City or Town: Durango

How to Get There: From Durango, take US-550 N/N. Main Ave. for 21 miles, and then turn right onto Electra Lake Rd. After Electra Lake Rd. becomes Electra East Rd., take a slight right onto Shober Dr. to reach the railroad.

GPS Coordinates: 37.2695° N, -107.8822° W

Did You Know? The steam engines on the D&SNG were originally built in the 1920s, and the diesel engines were built in the 1960s.

San Juan Skyway Scenic Byway

The Million Dollar Highway is just one stretch of the historic San Juan Skyway. If you have the time, it's definitely worth the 7-hour drive to see the byway in its entirety.

Start in Durango and drive through the history of Colorado as you stop in Telluride, Ouray, Silverton, and Ridgeway. You don't have to stay in the car the whole time, either. Hop on a train in Durango to explore the San Juan Mountains, or pull off at any of the numerous overlooks for a hike. Continue into and through Mesa Verde National Park, where many of the historic sites, including the cliff dwellings of the Ancestral Puebloans, overlap with the Trail of the Ancients Scenic Byway.

Best Time to Visit: Fall, when the autumn colors are at their peak, or spring, when the snow melts before the tourists arrive

Pass/Permit/Fees: None

Closest City or Town: Durango

How to Get There: From Durango, get onto US-550 S to enjoy a tour of the San Juan Skyway Scenic Byway. This route travels through the San Juan National Forest and continues on to Ouray.

GPS Coordinates: 37.7003° N, -107.7728° W

Did You Know? San Juan Skyway wasn't federally protected as a National Forest Scenic Byway until 1988.

Fulford Cave

Spelunkers cannot miss Fulford Cave. Although discovered over 150 years ago, Fulford still has many secret spots left to explore. The nearby campsites—aptly named Fulford Cave Campgrounds—give visitors a home base from which to explore the cave and the White River National Forest. The trailhead to the cave starts from the campgrounds and switchbacks through the forest of young aspens, and firs. You'll pass an active beaver pond and East Brush Creek. If you plan on entering the cave, follow the guidelines and caving rules posted by the U.S. Forest Service. Fulford Cave is home to Townsend's big-eared bats and the Myotis species of mouse-eared bats. It is closed annually from October 15 through April 15 during their hibernation season, and cavers are required to carry specialized and sterilized equipment to reduce the risks of the deadly White-Nose Syndrome. Permits are also required to enter the cave.

Best Time to Visit: June through October

Pass/Permit/Fees: Campsites cost between $15–$265 per night.

Closest City or Town: Eagle

How to Get There: From Eagle, take US-6 W/Grand Ave. to Sylvan Lake Rd. Turn right onto Bush Creek Rd., and the cave is in 16.4 miles.

GPS Coordinates: 39.4921° N, -106.6588° W

Did You Know? Fulford Cave is the eighth largest cave in Colorado.

Chasm Lake

Chasm Lake Trail is not intended for beginners. The nearly 9-mile round trip starts at the Longs Peak Ranger Station in Rocky Mountain National Park and ends at the glacial lake. Making it to the shores of Chasm Lake rewards hikers with an unmatched view of three famous peaks: Longs Peak, Mount Lady Washington, and Mount Meeker. You will experience an elevation gain of 2,500 feet, with an apex reaching 11,823 feet. The views don't really start until you're above the tree line about 2 miles in. For the best views—and if you want to reach the lake with enough time to enjoy lunch—plan on arriving at the trailhead before 5 a.m. The trail still sees snow in July, so dress appropriately and bring hiking poles. Micro-spikes are recommended.

Best Time to Visit: June to October. Reservations are required from May 28 through Oct 11.

Pass/Permit/Fees: $25 for a 1-day pass, $35 for a 7-day pass

Closest City or Town: Estes Park

How to Get There: From Estes Park, take N. St. Vrain Ave. to CO-7 E/S. St. Vrain Ave. In 9 miles, turn right onto Longs Peak Rd., and continue to stay on Longs Peak Road until you reach the Chasm Lake trailhead.

GPS Coordinates: 40.2583° N, -105.6050° W

Did You Know? If there's snow on the ground on your hike, you can expect Chasm Lake to be frozen over.

Dream Lake

For those willing to brave a winter's hike in Colorado, Dream Lake is the ideal destination. Hikers are wise to bring crampons, spikes, or snowshoes to the 1.1-mile hike on Bear Lake Trailhead. Arrive early in the morning before parking fills up. The hike is a little over 2 miles round trip, and the path forks off toward other destinations, including Lake Haiyaha and Emerald Lake. Dress appropriately and be prepared for severe weather conditions on the trail. Stop at Nymph Lake first, which is about half a mile into the trail. It may be small, but it's worth a glimpse, especially during the summer months when the water is covered with blooming pond lilies. Continue to Dream Lake for breathtaking views of Hallett Peak and Flattop Mountain, with a little sneak peek of the Tyndall Glacier. Head to Emerald Lake for a better view.

Best Time to Visit: April through November. Come early in the day to avoid crowds, especially on weekends.

Pass/Permit/Fees: $25 per vehicle, $15 per pedestrian

Closest City or Town: Estes Park

How to Get There: From Estes Park, head south on Park Ln. toward Virginia Dr. Turn right onto E. Elkhorn Ave. Turn left onto US-36 W/Moraine Ave. Take another left onto Bear Lake Rd. You'll reach Dream Lake in 9.4 miles.

GPS Coordinates: 40.3093° N, -105.6591° W

Did You Know? Snowshoes are the easiest way to get to Dream Lake during winter.

Longs Peak

Are you brave enough to take on the highest peak in Rocky Mountain National Park? Longs Peak is 14,259 high, and climbers face sheer vertical cliffs on their way to the summit. Even in winter, experienced ice climbers will still brave the peak. To reach the summit, take Keyhole Route, which starts at the Longs Peak Trailhead. Novice hikers should know that Longs Peak is not a normal hike, and experience is needed to safely climb the narrow ledges and loose rock. The Keyhole Route refers to the notch in the rocks hikers must cross through to continue their way to the summit. This "keyhole" is over 6 miles into the trailhead. It's home to the Agnes Vaille Shelter, a refuge for hikers in memoriam of Agnes Vaille, the first woman to climb the peak in winter only to die after a fall on her descent.

Best Time to Visit: July through September. Winter is too dangerous to climb Longs Peak.

Pass/Permit/Fees: There are no fees, but camping is limited to three days.

Closest City or Town: Estes Park

How to Get There: From Estes Park, follow CO-7 E/S. St. Vrain Ave for 9 miles to reach Longs Peak.

GPS Coordinates: 40.2549° N, -105.6160° W

Did You Know? Longs Peak is the most dangerous mountain in Colorado, responsible for 5 percent of the deaths in Rocky Mountain National Park. Nearly 70 percent of the deaths on Longs Peak are from falls.

Rocky Mountain National Park

With over 350 miles of trails, Rocky Mountain National Park is a hiker's dream. This park boasts the country's longest paved trails: Trail Ridge Road and Old Fall River Road. These scenic drives give visitors an intimate experience in nature without ever having to leave the car. Hikers will find lakes, waterfalls, and summit trails for all experience levels. For panoramic views, Peak 12,150 is an easy, well-defined trail for beginners, while the trek to Mt. Ida is a little longer and more rugged. Some areas of the tundra are closed to hiking and walking, so be aware and follow all park closure signs. Mountain biking and four-wheelers are welcome to explore the trails, but off-roading is not allowed. Horseback riding, fishing, and white-water rafting are other seasonal adventures.

Best Time to Visit: November through April is the best time to avoid crowds.

Pass/Permit/Fees: $25 per vehicle or $15 per pedestrian. Annual passes cost $70.

Closest City or Town: Estes Park

How to Get There: Head northeast on Park Ln. toward MacGregor Ave. Continue onto MacGregor Ave. Turn left at E. Wonderview Ave. Turn Left at MacGregor Ave. Take a slight right onto W. Wonderview Ave. Continue onto US-34 W until you reach the park. There are tolls on this route.

GPS Coordinates: 40.3428° N, -105.6836° W

Did You Know? Visitors can beat the crowds and enter the park without a reservation before 6 a.m. or after 5 p.m.

Trail Ridge Road

Trail Ridge Road is Rocky Mountain National Park's highway to the sky. Start in Estes Park and climb over 11,000 feet above the skyline. You'll pass through tundra at around 12,000 feet up that offers amazing views of the wildflowers in the spring. There are over 200 species of flora to see, and keep your eyes out for the fauna, too, including marmots, raptors, and bighorn sheep. Get out of your car and take a closer look at the Tundra World Nature Trail. It starts near Rock Cut and leads you on a 30-minute walk through wildflowers and wilderness. If you plan on leaving your car, dress appropriately. It is often 20–30 degrees colder at these altitudes, even in the summer, and you don't want a chilly wind to keep you from seeing all that there is up here.

Best Time to Visit: June through September is best.

Pass/Permit/Fees: Trail Ridge Road is in Rocky Mountain National Park, which costs $15 per person or $25 per vehicle to enter.

Closest City or Town: Estes Park

How to Get There: From Estes Park, head northeast on Park Ln. to MacGregor Ave. Take MacGregor Ave. to W. Wonderview Ave., and then continue onto US-34 W. You'll reach Trail Ridge Rd. in 17.9 miles.

GPS Coordinates: 40.3947° N, -105.7108° W

Did You Know? The Arapaho Indians referred to Trail Ridge as "Where the Children Walked" because it was too steep to carry them.

Two Rivers Lake

Reaching Two Rivers Lake in Rocky Mountain National Park is possible on either the Fern Lake Trailhead or the Bear Lake Trailhead. Break Lake is the shorter and easier route of the two and leads you to Odessa Lake, Flattop Mountain, and Lake Helene along the way.

Some hikers compare Two Rivers Lake to Lake Helene, and it's true that both are breathtakingly beautiful. But Two Rivers Lake sees considerably less foot traffic and gives you a more personal experience with Mother Nature.

To reach Two Rivers Lake, hug the tree line and head downstream from Lake Helene. A thick forest of trees and boulders will stand in your way, but the difficult terrain is worth it.

Best Time to Visit: Spring and summer offer the best weather for hiking and camping.

Pass/Permit/Fees: It will cost $15 per pedestrian or $25 per vehicle to enter Rocky Mountain National Park.

Closest City or Town: Estes Park

How to Get There: From Estes Park, head south on Park Ln. to reach E. Elkhorn Ave. Turn left onto US-36 W/Moraine Ave., and then take another left onto Bear Lake Rd. You'll reach the lake in 9.4 miles.

GPS Coordinates: 40.3213° N, -105.6825° W

Did You Know? Two Rivers Lake is one of the most popular spots to snowshoe in the state.

Horsetooth Reservoir

Horsetooth Reservoir is the place to be in Colorado during the summer. With over 6 miles of water to swim, fish, boat, and even scuba dive in, there's never a dull—or dry—moment. If you plan on camping, make sure you have a permit. If water isn't your thing, stay dry on the miles of hiking trails that surround the reservoir. The easiest trails are the Lake Access Trail, which is a little over a half-mile round trip, and Duncan's Ridge Trail, a short little jaunt that rewards visitors with a sweeping view of the reservoir and Horsetooth Rock. Rock climbers will get something extra at Duncan's Ridge: the sunniest spot to climb. It's also the closest rock climbing to Fort Collins and perfect for climbers of all skill levels.

Best Time to Visit: Visit between May and October to fish, hike, and camp in the best weather conditions.

Pass/Permit/Fees: $9, but Devil's Backbone Open Space is free

Closest City or Town: Fort Collins

How to Get There: From Fort Collins, take Dixon Canyon Rd. to Centennial Dr./S. County Rd. to reach the Horsetooth Reservoir.

GPS Coordinates: 40.5078° N, -105.1639° W

Did You Know? Native American legends tell the tale of a giant who was slain by Chief Maunamoku and later became Horsetooth Rock.

New Belgium Brewing Company

Take a tour of New Belgium Brewing Company and find out how their famous Fat Tire ale is born. Visitors can tour, taste, and shop on their own, or take advantage of the guided tours offered by the brewers themselves.

Guided tours are available for groups and can be customized for your unique event, but you don't need to take a tour to take a sip. Tastings are offered daily, and visitors are welcome to pick up their brews curbside. New Belgium also hosts numerous events throughout the year, featuring live music, brunch specials, and food trucks.

Although you must be over 21 to drink, New Belgium is family-friendly and encourages visitors to bring their own snacks and picnics to enjoy with their brews.

Best Time to Visit: September through October when you can enjoy the brewery's outdoor space

Pass/Permit/Fees: Tours are free but fill up quickly.

Closest City or Town: Fort Collins

How to Get There: In Fort Collins, head north on Sherwood St. Turn right onto Cherry St., then left on Linden St. to reach the brewery at 500 Linden St.

GPS Coordinates: 40.5932° N, -105.0686° W

Did You Know? The famous Fat Tire recipe was developed when founders Kim Jordan and Jeff Lebesch took a biking brewery tour throughout Belgium.

Campe Diem

If perfection were a campsite, it would be Campe Diem. The peace and serenity found here are unmatched, but if you crave adventure, you won't be disappointed. Take a dip in the reservoir or head out on a four-wheeler tour to explore the 65 acres of campground. Stretch your legs on a hike into Fort Garland, or take a day trip to the Great Sand Dunes National Park. The backcountry sites require campers to bring their own equipment, and firewood must be purchased on site, but you're also welcome to bring four-wheelers, jet skis, and pets. Campsites are available across multiple comfortable plateaus with views of different landscapes, depending on where you decide to pitch your tent.

Due to the backcountry nature of the site, Campe Diem is best for experienced campers and hikers.

Best Time to Visit: The summer months are the mildest for camping.

Pass/Permit/Fees: Passes start at $30 per night.

Closest City or Town: Fort Garland

How to Get There: From Fort Garland, take CO-159 S to County Lane 6. Turn left onto Garson Rd., and then left onto Butchy Rd. to reach the camp.

GPS Coordinates: 37.3702° N, -105.3772° W

Did You Know? Campsites at Campe Diem are often considered primitive campsites because they are not outfitted with amenities.

Georgetown Loop

Immerse yourself in the Rocky Mountains with a train ride on the Georgetown Loop Railroad. It's a trip back in time. The narrow rail ride mimics the mining rails of the 1880s, and the living museum nearby allows visitors to explore a silver mine and learn how to pan for gold.

If you can, book a ride on the famed Georgetown caboose for the best views. The caboose was originally built in 1885 and spent nearly a century carrying pioneers, miners, and supplies across the Denver and Rio Grande railroads. Seats fill up quickly, so book ahead of time to get a spot.

It only takes 1 hour and 15 minutes to get up close and personal with Colorado history on the Georgetown Loop, and if you include the mining tour, the experience will take a little over 2 hours.

Best Time to Visit: April through December, but the best time to ride is summer or early autumn

Pass/Permit/Fees: Tickets start at $3.

Closest City or Town: Georgetown

How to Get There: In Georgetown, head west on Sixth St., and take a slight left onto Loop Dr. to reach the Georgetown Loop Railroad at 646 Loop Dr.

GPS Coordinates: 39.7010° N, -105.7068° W

Did You Know? At least seven trains would pass through Georgetown Loop per day during its peak in the late 19th century.

Guanella Pass Scenic Byway

Hop in your car and take a drive cut snugly between two national forests: Arapaho National Forest and Pike National Forest. The road is paved the entire way, so you won't need a four-wheeler, but the turns are tight and high.

Guanella Pass is not for the faint of heart. You will climb to 11,669 feet over the course of 12 miles, completing the drive in a little over an hour unless you get out to hike or camp along the byway.

Mount Bierstadt and Mt. Evans are two popular peaks to stop and hike, but these 14-mile routes are no stroll through the woods. Be prepared to carve out 3–6 hours of your day to really enjoy the hikes on Guanella Pass.

Best Time to Visit: October and September are the best times to cruise the byway. The road is not maintained during the winter and will likely be closed from November through February.

Pass/Permit/Fees: None. The drive is free, but campgrounds may require reservations.

Closest City or Town: Georgetown

How to Get There: From Georgetown, head east on Sixth St. to Rose St., and then turn left onto Guanella Pass Rd./Second St. Check for closures before planning a trip.

GPS Coordinates: 39.8404° N, -105.5291° W

Did You Know? The bypass once led to a ski resort known as Geneva Basin, which operated from 1963–1984.

Glenwood Hot Springs Pool

Don't be discouraged by the smell of eggs—that's just the sulfur at work beneath the Glenwood Hot Springs Pool. You'll forget the smell as soon as you take a dip. Visitors have the choice of soaking it up in the bigger pool that's kept at a comfortable 90°F, or the therapy pool, which is smaller and hotter at 104°F, but perfect for relaxing stiff muscles and sore joints. As you soak in the springs, that stinky sulfur heals your skin, helping it build collagen and strengthen your hair and fingernails. On top of the sulfur, there are 15 more minerals at work in the hot springs. Reservations are not required at Glenwood, but the pool fills up quickly on a first-come, first-served basis. Guests staying at the Glenwood Hot Springs Resort can rent their own cabanas.

Best Time to Visit: Spring and winter. The pools close a few hours daily for cleaning and maintenance.

Pass/Permit/Fees: $16.25 per adult, $10.75 for children 12 and under

Closest City or Town: Glenwood Springs

How to Get There: While in Glenwood Springs, head south on Pine St. to 6th St., then take a slight right onto N. River St. The hot springs are on the right at 401 N. River St.

GPS Coordinates: 39.5497° N, -107.3223° W

Did You Know? Yampah springs and vapor caves, which feed the hot spring, are the only naturally occurring vapor caves in North America.

Hanging Lake

Hanging Lake flows from Glenwood Canyon, the largest canyon in northern Colorado. Shuttle service brings visitors to the lake from May through October. Personal vehicles are not allowed during this time, but biking and hiking to the lake via the Glenwood Canyon Recreation Path are still permitted. The hike to and from Hanging Lake is a little over 3 miles, but it is steep and slippery. Novice hikers should not hike alone, and even an experienced hiker must be prepared. Shoes with good tread, hiking poles, and plenty of water are recommended. The trail to Hanging Lake is designed to protect the canyon from erosion, pollution, and other threats to local flora and fauna. Swimming is not allowed at Hanging Lake, but the trail leads hikers around the water.

Best Time to Visit: April through October. Hiking during winter is not recommended due to the difficulty of the trail.

Pass/Permit/Fees: Hikers need a permit to access the lake. Permits are $12 per person.

Closest City or Town: Glenwood Springs

How to Get There: From Glenwood Springs, take CO-82 W to I-70 E. In 0.2 miles, take exit 129 toward Bair Ranch. In another 0.2 miles, take a sharp left. Merge onto I-70 W, and Hanging Lake is in 2.3 miles.

GPS Coordinates: 39.0164° N, -107.1918° W

Did You Know? This natural wonder is called the "Hanging" Lake because of the beautiful waterfall and the dense gardens haloing the lake.

Buffalo Bill Museum and Grave

William Frederick Cody, better known as Buffalo Bill, is an American war hero, having served the Union in the Civil War and earning the Medal of Honor in the Indian Wars. But his nickname didn't come from his heroics. Buffalo Bill was known for supplying American forces with bison meat; his hunting skills were unmatched. Legend says he killed over 4,200 buffalo in 18 months. The Buffalo Bill Museum offers an up-close-and-personal look at Buffalo Bill's life and the lives of others in the Wild West. There are many permanent exhibits, including a hands-on cowboy corral for the kids, and various traveling exhibits that visit every year. The most famous element is Buffalo Bill's grave. It was his choice to be buried on Lookout Mountain, and you can take in that same view after touring the museum.

Best Time to Visit: It is best to visit February to March.

Pass/Permit/Fees: $5 for adults, $4 for seniors, $1 for children, and free for children under five

Closest City or Town: Golden

How to Get There: In Golden, head southwest on 12th St. to get onto Washington Ave. Turn right onto 19th St., and then continue onto Lookout Mountain Rd. for 4.4 miles to reach the museum.

GPS Coordinates: 39.7334° N, -105.2385° W

Did You Know? Buffalo Bill never lived in Denver but visited numerous times, starting with the Pikes Peak Gold Rush in 1859.

Clear Creek

If you're visiting Colorado during the summer, a trip to Clear Creek is almost mandatory. It is a kayaker's dream, and there are also plenty of opportunities for tubing and white-water rafting of all skill levels. Or stay dry and hit any number of the hiking and biking trails around the creek. If you do plan on getting in the water, pay attention to the creek warning flags. Flag warnings change as the flow of the creek increases, typically during the spring snowmelt. If conditions are dangerous, children are not allowed in the water, or the creek may be closed to the public. Camping is allowed around Clear Creek. Some campgrounds are only open between Memorial Day and Labor Day. Visitors wishing to camp all year can take advantage of the public campgrounds, RV campgrounds, yurts, and cabins in nearby Clear Creek County.

Best Time to Visit: June through October

Pass/Permit/Fees: Free, but permits are required for events

Closest City or Town: Golden

How to Get There: From Golden, take CO-58 E and use Exit 5A to merge onto I-70 toward Denver. Take Exit 269B for I-76 E, and then take Exit 1B to get on CO-95 S/Sheridan Blvd. Turn left onto W. 52nd Ave., and then left onto Tennyson St. to reach Clear Creek.

GPS Coordinates: 39.6904° N, -105.6413° W

Did You Know? If you get lost, Clear Creek ambassadors are posted along the water on the weekends to help you find your way.

Colorado Railroad Museum

The depot museum, railyard, roundhouse, and library all make up the Colorado Railroad Museum. You can easily spend the whole day here learning the history of Colorado's railways and taking rides on the vintage steam engines around the museum grounds. The 15-acre railyard is the best part, boasting over 100 different steam and diesel engines, cabooses, passenger cars, and a vintage roundhouse with a working turntable. Roundhouses once acted as garages to repair and maintain train cars and engines, and visitors can watch trains move in and out of the historic facility. During the holidays, the Colorado Railroad Museum hosts different events for families, children, and adults, but there are learning opportunities for kids of all ages offered all year round.

Best Time to Visit: Thursday through Sunday when train rides are available. In the winter (January through May), train rides are only offered on Saturdays.

Pass/Permit/Fees: $10 for adults, $8 for seniors, $5 for children

Closest City or Town: Golden

How to Get There: In Golden, head northeast on 12th St. and turn left onto Ford St. Take a right onto 10th St. and continue until you reach the museum at 17155 W. 44th Ave.

GPS Coordinates: 39.7715° N, -105.1934° W

Did You Know? The museum got its start when founder Robert W. Richardson began to collect artifacts as railroad companies went out of business in the 1940s.

Kawuneeche Valley

Kawuneeche Valley is one of the most popular spots in Rocky Mountain National Park. It's home to amazing wildlife and epic mountain scenery and is every hiker's dream. Hiking trails in Kawuneeche Valley lead to some of the best-hidden gems in the park. The easiest trails take hikers to Adams Falls (East Inlet Trailhead) and Cascade Trails (North Inlet Trailhead). Get a historical tour of Lulu City, a ghost town in the middle of the Colorado River Trailhead, or snap a picture of Timber Lake on the Timber Lake trailhead.

Most of these hikes will take less than 4 hours round trip, but visitors are welcome to stay overnight and camp along the Colorado River. Fly-fishing is popular in the summer, and campers love to visit in the early spring to catch the wildflowers in bloom.

Best Time to Visit: November through April

Pass/Permit/Fees: $15 per person, $25 per vehicle

Closest City or Town: Granby

How to Get There: From Granby, take US-34 E. In 14.4 miles, turn left onto County Rd. 491/US National Park Rd. to reach Kawuneeche Valley.

GPS Coordinates: 40.2833° N, -105.8506° W

Did You Know? Kawuneeche Valley is also known as Coyote Valley and is one of the best places to catch sight of coyotes, moose, and elk in Colorado.

Lake Granby

Visiting Lake Granby means visiting three lakes at once. Lake Granby shares over 40 miles worth of shoreline with its sisters Grand Lake and Shadow Mountain Lake, offering up plenty of room for swimming, fishing, and boating.

Boating can get competitive in the summer courtesy of the Granby Yacht Club's boat racing, but don't worry—there is plenty of space for leisure sailors, kayakers, and paddle boarders, too. And since the lake is right in the middle of the Arapaho National Recreation Area and the Indian Peaks Wilderness, you'll never feel too crowded.

Get lost at Lake Granby with over 250 campsites, white-water rafting tours, horseback riding, and more. You'll never run out of things to do. Even in the winter, snowshoeing and snowmobiling are must-do activities, and skiers can hit the slopes at nearby Ski Granby Ranch.

Best Time to Visit: June through September

Pass/Permit/Fees: $5 daily pass

Closest City or Town: Granby

How to Get There: From Granby, take County Hwy. 61 to US-34 E, and then turn right onto County Hwy. 6. Lake Granby is on the left.

GPS Coordinates: 40.1481° N, -105.8658° W

Did You Know? The Granby Yacht Club is the highest in the country, sitting at 8,280 feet above sea level.

Lone Eagle Peak

Lone Eagle Peak is nestled neatly in the Indian Peaks Wilderness, making it a challenging mountain to get to. The hike to Lone Eagle starts on the Monarch Lake Trailhead and continues over 14 miles to waterfalls, lakes, and eventually the summit. The trail is clearly marked, and hikers will pass many junctions. Follow signs for Cascade Creek and Crater Lake. When you pass Cascade Falls, your first sights of Lone Eagle Peak will be coming up. Continue following signs for Crater Lake to reach the peak.

There are backcountry campsites along the trailhead, but every visitor needs a permit to camp overnight or they will face hefty fines. If you don't want to stay overnight, the Cascade Creek trail is accessible by vehicle, which shortens the hike into a day trip by dropping hikers off past Crater Lake.

Best Time to Visit: Backpacking permits are required from June to September during the best time to visit.

Pass/Permit/Fees: Free to hike, $5 to park, $5 per camping permit

Closest City or Town: Granby

How to Get There: From Granby, take US-34 E for 3.9 miles, and then turn right onto Co Hwy. The Monarch Lake Trailhead will be on the right in 9.7 miles.

GPS Coordinates: 40.0714° N, -105.6603° W

Did You Know? Lone Eagle Peak was previously called "Lindbergh Peak" or "Mount Lindbergh."

Monarch Lake

Monarch Lake is your chance to swim in the prettiest lake in Colorado. No motorized boats are allowed, but water lovers can hop into a kayak or just dive in for a swim. The secret to Monarch Lake isn't the water—it's the hiking trails.

There are over 30 miles of trails throughout the Monarch Wilderness area, and the most popular is Monarch Lake Loop Trail, a 4-mile easy hike around the water that offers up the best views right from the beginning. The trailhead branches off to the Cascade Creek Trail and the High Lonesome Trail. More experienced hikers can explore the Indian Peaks Wilderness Area via the Continental Divide Trail. If you plan on camping, permits are required for overnight stays. Campsites dot the Monarch Lake Loop Trail, and reservations are recommended, especially during the summer when the lake is most crowded.

Best Time to Visit: June through September

Pass/Permit/Fees: $5 per day

Closest City or Town: Granby

How to Get There: From Granby, take US-34 E to County Hwy. 6, and the Monarch Lake Trailhead is in 9.6 miles.

GPS Coordinates: 40.1045° N, -105.7395° W

Did You Know? The Monarch Wilderness area is home to the largest groves of Giant Sequoias outside of Sequoia-Kings Canyon.

Colorado National Monument

Rim Rock Drive is the only paved road through the Colorado National Monument, and it's an excellent place to start. Road bikers follow the Colorado River up to the Uncompahgre Plateau. Take in the canyon views and choose your next route on the Lunch Loops Trails. The advanced system of trails at the Colorado National Monument varies in degrees of difficulty, so bikers and hikers of all levels can enjoy the scenery. If you want to get into the backcountry, ditch the bike and hike on foot.

For a more historical perspective, take the 3.4-mile Serpents Trail, which is the original path into the Colorado National Monument. Serpents Trail leads to the Pipe Organ formation, and you can loop the Window Rock Trail for a view of Wedding Canyon.

Best Time to Visit: Any time before June is the best time to visit.

Pass/Permit/Fees: $25 per vehicle, $15 per pedestrian

Closest City or Town: Grand Junction

How to Get There: From Grand Junction, take Ute Ave, which turns slightly right and becomes S. 1st St. In 0.3 miles, turn left onto W. Grand Ave. Continue onto Broadway in 0.1 miles, then turn left onto Monument Rd. You'll arrive at the monument in 3.4 miles.

GPS Coordinates: 39.0575° N, -108.6939° W

Did You Know? The first park ranger for Colorado National Monument earned $1 per month.

Grand Lake

If you were to stand in Estes Park, Grand Lake is directly across the other side of Rocky Mountain National Park. It's only 90 minutes from Estes Park to Grand Lake, so it's possible to make a day trip between the two iconic spots. Grand Lake offers up the deepest lake in Colorado, complete with public boat ramps and docks. Join in on the summer fun with fishing and sailing, or hit the trails on foot, by bike, or via four-wheeler. In winter, you can still explore the outdoors with snowshoes or take advantage of the 21 miles of Nordic ski trails. Stay warm with some local food and shopping on the boardwalk, and don't miss out on the ice rink that opens on Grand Avenue every winter from December through February.

Best Time to Visit: May through July. Come during spring to avoid the summer crowds.

Pass/Permit/Fees: If you plan on visiting Rocky Mountain National Park, it is $25 per vehicle and $15 per pedestrian for day passes.

Closest City or Town: Grand Lake

How to Get There: From Vine St., turn right onto Lake Ave. and take a slight left onto Cairns St. Turn right onto Lakeside Dr., then left onto Jericho Rd. You'll reach Point Park on the lake's shore at 1121 3rd St.

GPS Coordinates: 40.2459° N, -105.8258° W

Did You Know? There may be gold hidden somewhere in the city left behind by The Hermit of Grand Lake.

Shadow Mountain Lake

Hit the water in a powerboat, on a jet ski, or in a kayak or canoe. There are two boat launches at the Green Ridge campground by the lake for your convenience. Green Ridge is a non-electric campsite but offers other amenities, including restrooms, drinking water, and trash services.

Are you looking for a place to relax? Head to Lake Granby or any of the creeks and rivers in between to find a quiet place to fish, sleep, or swim.

For the landlubbers, Shadow Mountain Lake offers the East Shore Trail, which boasts a sneak peek of the longer Continental Divide National Scenic Trail nearby or the Shadow Mountain Trail, which leads right up to the fire lookout and some amazing views.

Best Time to Visit: The lake is open all year round, but visit in summer and early fall to enjoy swimming, boating, and fishing on the lake.

Pass/Permit/Fees: $5 recreation fee

Closest City or Town: Grand Lake

How to Get There: From Grand Lake, use W. Portal Rd. to get on US-34 W/Trail Ridge Rd. In 2 miles, take a sharp left to reach the lake.

GPS Coordinates: 40.2261° N, -105.8437° W

Did You Know? Dogs are allowed at Shadow Mountain Lake but must remain on a leash.

Pearl Lake State Park

Pearl Lake State Park sits comfortably at the base of Hahns Peak, blessing visitors with breathtaking views while offering up some of the best water activities and fly-fishing opportunities in the state. Two unique yurts dot the campgrounds and come equipped with heat and electricity, making them a snug spot to sleep in the winter. All campsites are within walking distance of the reservoir, and hikers can venture further around the water via the Pearl Lake Connection Trail. For a longer hike, Pearl Lake Connection Trail will connect with Coulton Creek Trail in the Routt National Forest. Most of Pearl Lake closes during the winter, but there are plenty of opportunities to hike, cross-country ski, and ice fish. Trails are not maintained in winter, and backcountry experience is recommended.

Best Time to Visit: May through September. Campgrounds are closed during the winter, but the yurts are open.

Pass/Permit/Fees: $9 per vehicle, $4 per pedestrian, $80 annual pass

Closest City or Town: Hahns Peak Village

How to Get There: From Hahns Peak Village, head southeast on County Rd. 129 toward Cottonwood Dr./Main St. In 2 miles, turn left onto County Rd. 209, and you'll arrive at the park in 2.1 miles at 61105 Rcr 129.

GPS Coordinates: 40.7871° N, -106.8872° W

Did You Know? The park is named after Pearl Hartt, who sold the land to the U.S. Forest Service.

John Martin Reservoir State Park

Get ready to hit the water! During the summer, the lake at John Martin Reservoir State Park is rarely as crowded as the other Colorado lakes. There's plenty of room on the water to fish, sail, jet ski, and water ski. If you have an eye out for wildlife, take the Red Shin Hiking Trail. The 4.5-mile path leads through the park, along the water, and to the Santa Fe Historic Site, with ample opportunities to spot deer, coyote, and prairie dogs.

Bring your binoculars to catch sight of the 400 different species of birds living in the park. You might even spy a bald eagle. Beyond wildlife, the hiking trails at John Martin take visitors back in time to a historic ranch from the 19th century and even further to the ancient petroglyphs left behind by the tribes who hunted buffalo in the area.

Best Time to Visit: April through September. Campgrounds are closed during winter.

Pass/Permit/Fees: $9 per vehicle, $17–28 to camp

Closest City or Town: Hasty

How to Get There: From Hasty, head west on E. Park Ave., and then take a left on S. School St. In 1.5 miles, you'll reach the park at 30703 County Road 24.

GPS Coordinates: 38.0794° N, -103.0319° W

Did You Know? Red Shin Trail is named for a warrior from the Cheyenne Tribe who defended his honor atop the Dakota Sandstone formation.

Argo Gold Mine and Mill

A tour of the Argo is more than just a mining tour. Visitors will tour the gold mine, refining mill, and the historical tunnel that made it possible for the Argo to become one of Colorado's largest and most famous gold mills.

The Argo Mill was responsible for processing over $100 million worth of gold ore during the late 1890s. The ore came from the Argo Mine as well as mines in Virginia Canyon, Nevadaville, Central City, and other surrounding areas. That amount translates to $2.6 trillion today.

See the history unfold before you with a peek inside the Argo Tunnel portal and a closer look at the larger-than-life machinery used to process gold back then. Take a unique opportunity to pan for gold like a real prospector.

Best Time to Visit: Spring and summer. Tours are not available during the winter.

Pass/Permit/Fees: Tours cost $25 for adults, $20 for children over 4, and $4 for children 4 and under. Panning without a tour costs $12-$16 per person.

Closest City or Town: Idaho Springs

How to Get There: In Idaho Springs, head northeast on Riverside Dr. toward Twenty-Second Ave. to reach the Gold Mill at 2350 Riverside Dr.

GPS Coordinates: 39.7427° N, -105.5067° W

Did You Know? A catastrophic flood in the famous Argo Tunnel closed the mine in 1943.

Mount Evans Scenic Byway

The trip up to the 14,260-foot peak of Mount Evans is full of twists, turns, and sweeping views of the Rocky Mountains. If you're afraid of heights, stay away—many spots don't have guardrails. If you can brave it, start the Mount Evans Scenic Byway from Echo Lake. After 3 miles, the byway breaks above the trees.

Stop at the Walter Pesman Alpine Garden for a closer look. Take a hike out of the car on Mount Goliath or Summit Trails. There are guided tours during the summer months, or experienced hikers can traverse the tundra on their own. Summit Lake is one of the last stops on the way to Mount Evans. Follow the quarter-mile trail to the top of the mountain, and keep an eye out for the mountain goats that hang out around the cliffs and wildflowers.

Best Time to Visit: Summer. The best times for a drive are weekday mornings. Part of the byway is closed during winter.

Pass/Permit/Fees: $10 per vehicle, $5 to park

Closest City or Town: Idaho Springs

How to Get There: From Idaho Springs, take CO-103 S toward Echo Lake. In 13.1 miles, turn right onto CO-5 S. The byway will be on the left in 14.3 miles.

GPS Coordinates: 39.5884° N, -105.6440° W

Did You Know? Don't forget your sunscreen! At this altitude, there is 50 percent less protection from the sun.

Lake San Cristobal

Lake San Cristobal is one of the only lakes in the country with a naturally formed dam caused by a mudslide that happened over 700 years ago. While other natural lakes will need their dams reinforced, Lake San Cristobal's is carved into the bedrock and will last for more than 2,500 years. Thanks to Mother Nature, visitors today can jump into the lake for a swim, hit the shores for some fishing, or hop on a boat. Campers can set up tents at the Wupperman Campground nearby or just enjoy the day with a picnic at the Red Mountain Gulch Day Use Area. If you hit the trails, keep your eyes peeled for the array of wildlife that is attracted to the water. Raptors, migratory birds, elk, moose, and beaver can pop up at any time, and you won't want to miss them.

Best Time to Visit: Spring, Fall, and Winter attract smaller crowds.

Pass/Permit/Fees: Lake San Cristobal is free to visit, but it costs $15 per night to camp. Fishing licenses are required.

Closest City or Town: Lake City

How to Get There: From Lake City, head south on CO-149 S/Gunnison Ave. Turk right onto County Rd. 30, and then left onto County Rd. 33 to reach Lake San Cristobal.

GPS Coordinates: 37.9757° N, -107.2888° W

Did You Know? Lake City legend Alferd Packer was jailed for killing and cannibalizing his fellow prospectors in 1874, and the skeletal remains are on display in the nearby Hinsdale County Museum.

Turquoise Lake

Turquoise Lake, which sits 9,800 feet above sea level, is situated between Colorado's two highest peaks: Mount Elbert and Mount Massive. This makes the lake literally one of the coolest spots to be in the middle of summer. Escape the heat by boating, swimming, or fishing. The summer season is quick, only lasting from June to September, so soak up the sun when you can. In winter, the roads and paths around the lake are maintained weekly for snowmobiling and Nordic skiing. Some hiking trails remain open in the winter, but bring your snowshoes or bike. The paved paths are maintained all year round, and the paved road around the lake leads to epic overlooks of the peaks and water.

Best Time to Visit: Summer is the best time to swim, but winter offers up ice fishing and fewer crowds on the water.

Pass/Permit/Fees: There are no fees to visit, but fishing licenses are required for anyone over 16.

Closest City or Town: Leadville

How to Get There: From Leadville, head south on Harrison Ave. and turn right at the first cross street onto W. 8th St. Turn right onto James St., and stay on James St. until you can take a left onto McWethy Dr. Turn right onto County Rd. 4, and stay right to reach Turquoise Lake Rd.

GPS Coordinates: 39.2713° N, -106.3788° W

Did You Know? Turquoise Lake is not named for its beautiful waters but for the turquoise that once washed up on its shores before the mines.

Chatfield State Park

Chatfield State Park is *the* spot for water sports for anyone visiting from the Denver area. The 1,500-acre reservoir is more extensive than most in Colorado, and the water is open to most types of water vehicles, including powerboats, sailboats, and jet skis. Visitors are allowed to swim in the reservoir from Memorial Day weekend through Labor Day weekend, and campsites are open through mid-October. Get out of the water and hit one of the hundreds of trails open to hikers, bikers, and horseback riding. There are 26 miles of biking trails, half of which are paved, and another 24 miles of horseback-riding trails with a stable right there in the park.

Best Time to Visit: May through September. The park is open all year round and gets crowded quickly. If you are not camping overnight, come to the park before 9 a.m. or after 4 p.m.

Pass/Permit/Fees: $10 per vehicle, $80 annual pass

Closest City or Town: Littleton

How to Get There: From Littleton, follow S. Santa Fe Dr. to CO-470 W. Take Exit 14 for CO-121 S. From Denver, take US-85 S and merge onto CO-470 W. Take Exit 14 for CO-121 S. The park is located on the left at 11500 N. Roxborough Park Rd.

GPS Coordinates: 39.5431° N, -105.0648° W

Did You Know? The Chatfield Dam at the reservoir was created after deadly floods destroyed the area in 1933, 1935, 1942, and 1965.

Roxborough State Park

With hiking trails as short as 1.5 miles, Roxborough State Park is the perfect place for a quick hike that won't take up the entire day. It is designated as an Important Bird Area, so bring your binoculars. Take advantage of the naturalist-guided hikes offered by the park, or explore on your own. Follow the Willow Creek Trail (1.5 miles) in a loop through the red rock formations. The Carpenter Peak Trail is a 6.2-mile hike to the top of Carpenter Peak, which will reward you with sweeping views of the Fountain Formations juxtaposed with the city of Denver.

Best Time to Visit: April through September. However, the park is open all year round. Bring snowshoes in the winter.

Pass/Permit/Fees: $10 per vehicle, $4 per pedestrian, $80 annual pass

Closest City or Town: Littleton

How to Get There: From Littleton, take CO-75 S/S. Platte Canyon Rd. In 3.2 miles, take the third exit at the traffic circle onto CO-470 W ramp to C-470. Use Exit 14 for CO-121 S, and then turn left onto CO-121 S/S. Wadsworth Blvd. Take another left onto Waterton Rd. in 4.4 miles. In 1.6 miles, turn right onto N. Rampart Range Rd., and then turn left onto Roxborough Dr. Stay on Roxborough Dr., and you'll find two parking lots on the right.

GPS Coordinates: 39.4296° N, -105.0691° W

Did You Know? The famous Fountain Formations of red sandstone are 300 million years old.

Black Canyon of the Gunnison

Have a need for speed? Take a scenic drive through the Black Canyon of the Gunnison National Park to catch sight of the Gunnison River speeding down the face of the cliff. This river flows down the mountain faster than any other river in North America, and the national park is home to one of the fastest birds in the world: the peregrine falcon.

Black Canyon National Park has two sides to explore. The South Rim is more developed for novice hikers, while the North Rim is rugged with epic views of the canyon. There is no bridge linking the rims, so give yourself at least three hours to drive from one edge to the other. Stop for the 1-mile hike on Rim Rock Nature Trail or a 2-mile hike with a view from just below the canyon rim on Oak Flat Loop Trail.

Best Time to Visit: Summer is ideal. The northern access roads are closed from November–April.

Pass/Permit/Fees: $30 per vehicle for seven days, $15 per pedestrian, or annual passes for $55

Closest City or Town: Montrose

How to Get There: From Montrose, take US-50 E to CO-347 N toward South Rim Rd. From Grand Junction, take US-50 E through G50 Rd. to CO-347 N.

GPS Coordinates: 38.5754° N, -107.7416° W

Did You Know? The exposed Precambrian rock in Black Canyon is over two billion years old.

South Rim Road

You will have your choice of 12 overlooks when you take the South Rim Road around Gunnison National Park. The first is right at the visitor's center and offers up a bird's-eye view into the depths of the canyon. Give yourself at least 3 hours to see all that you want to see along the South Rim. Be aware that some of these overlooks are a little way into the woods, and you may have to do a bit of walking to earn your view of the mountains in some spots. The longest lookout will be Devil's Lookout, which is about 1.4 miles from the road and can take 30 minutes to reach. Others are right off the road or conveniently located near a parking lot.

Best Time to Visit: The road is only open from April through November. The best time for a drive is May, September, or October.

Pass/Permit/Fees: South Rim is free, but the entrance to Gunnison National Park is $15 per person or $30 per vehicle.

Closest City or Town: Montrose

How to Get There: From Montrose, head northeast on S. 1st St. until you reach S. Cascade Ave. From S. Cascade Ave., turn right onto E. Main St. and continue onto US-50 E. In 5.8 miles, turn left onto CO-347 N, which will turn into South Rim Road in 5.2 miles.

GPS Coordinates: 36.3128° N, -112.1252° W

Did You Know? If you brave the narrow East Portal Road, you'll find pristine campsites and primitive trails.

Jackson Lake State Park

Jump into the 2,700-acre reservoir at Jackson Lake State Park. Stay on the shore at one of the park's many waterside campsites or visit during the winter for a quiet day of ice fishing and skating. Hike or bike the quarter-mile Prairie Wetland Nature Trail for an inside look at prairie ecosystems and wildlife. Campers can take the 1.5-mile path from the visitor center to reach the Northview Campground. Are you looking for something more action-packed? Hit the off-roading track. Off-highway vehicles (OHV) and four-wheelers are not allowed on park roads or in the campgrounds, but the 1.5-mile track gives visitors a glimpse of the prairie, even at top speed. The OHV track is open until sunset.

Best Time to Visit: The park is open all year round, but some campsites start to close for the winter in October.

Pass/Permit/Fees: $9 per vehicle, $80 annual pass, $28–$36 per campsite

Closest City or Town: Morgan County

How to Get There: From Morgan County, take State Hwy. 52 W to 1-76 W. Use Exit 66A to reach CO-39 N. Turn left onto County Rd. Y 5/10, then continue onto County Rd. 3/County Rd. 300. Take a right and then the lake will be on the left at 26363 County Rd. 3.

GPS Coordinates: 40.3847° N, -104.0916° W

Did You Know? The Jackson Lake reservoir area was initially inhabited by Sioux, Cheyenne, and Arapahoe Native American tribes.

Red Rocks Amphitheater

Red Rocks Amphitheater is a naturally formed open-air theater, testament to the artistic strength of Mother Nature. Take a seat snuggled between Ship Rock and Creation Rock, the two formations that make up the amphitheater, and enjoy the view. These monoliths are 300 feet high, and the seating is over 6,000 feet above sea level. While some come to see their favorite bands, Red Rocks Amphitheater is a park first and foremost. Hikers can hit the Trading Post Trail, or take the Red Rocks Trail on foot, by bike, or on horseback. Visitors can take self-guided tours, and nearby Dinosaur Ridge offers simulated archeological digs and historical exhibits.

Best Time to Visit: March through November

Pass/Permit/Fees: None, but events will have individual ticket prices

Closest City or Town: Morrison

How to Get There: From Morrison, head northeast on Bear Creek Ave./Morrison Rd. Turn right onto Red Rocks Park Rd., and then take a slight left onto Ship Rocks Rd. From Ship Rocks Rd., you can access Trading Post Rd. and Red Rocks Park Rd. There are four parking lots and multiple trails between them.

GPS Coordinates: 39.6655° N, -105.2052° W

Did You Know? Red Rocks Amphitheater was formerly known as "The Garden of the Angels" and "The Garden of the Titans."

Medano Creek

Medano Creek is your chance to see the infamous surge flow at the Great Sand Dunes National Park. Typically, the creek is barely wider than 20 feet and is never deeper than a few inches, but the exact width and depth depend on the snowmelt from the mountains.

At its peak, it's possible to float down the creek on an inner tube. The surge will carry you quite far, and the water temperature will be just right. Any warmer and the mosquitoes might just eat you alive.

May and June are the only time to see the Medano Creek surge unless there are heavy rains—then, you can expect the surge to flow into the first week of July. But because the timing of the surge is so short, you can expect parking lots and campgrounds to fill up quickly. Ride the surge on a weekday to avoid the summer crowds.

Best Time to Visit: Medano Creek doesn't typically flow before April or after July.

Pass/Permit/Fees: $25 per vehicle, $15 per pedestrian

Closest City or Town: Mosca

How to Get There: From Mosca, start on Lane 6 N, then turn left onto County Rd. 150 N. In 6.8 miles, the creek will be on the left.

GPS Coordinates: 37.7125° N, -105.5705° W

Did You Know? Avoid mosquitoes by staying in the sun. Bugs don't like the heat on the open sand.

Zapata Falls

When it comes to waterfalls, the hike to Zapata Falls is one of the easiest. Fording a stream and a few slippery rocks on a narrow log bridge is worth it to watch a waterfall against the backdrop of the Great Sand Dunes, especially if you hit the trail at sunrise or sunset.

The trail to Zapata Falls is just under 1 mile long and starts right in the parking lot, about 8 miles away from Great Sand Dune National Park. The hike is short—but rocky and wet—so spikes and closed-toed shoes are a must.

Zapata Falls is remotely located, so visitors should consider making a trip to the Great Sand Dune National Park or staying to camp near the Zapata Falls Trailhead overnight to make the most of the hike.

Best Time to Visit: Take a hike in the spring for premium birdwatching, or come during winter to catch ice climbers on the falls.

Pass/Permit/Fees: Free to hike and visit, $11 per night to camp

Closest City or Town: Mosca

How to Get There: From Mosca, take Lane 6 N, then turn right on CO-150 S. In 2.8 miles, turn left. Zapata Campground Loop will be on the right.

GPS Coordinates: 37.6189° N, -105.5531° W

Did You Know? Black swifts build their nests in the mists of the falls. Be careful not to disturb them.

Mount Princeton Hot Springs

Weary miners and travelers started soaking in Mount Princeton Hot Springs in the early 1800s, and the Ute Indians camped in the area during the winter months. Travelers still stay in the cozy comforts of cabins, suites, or cliffside rooms. The resort boasts a 400-foot water slide and multiple pools. Mount Princeton Hot Springs is surrounded by the San Isabel National Forest along with hiking and backpacking trails. Book horseback riding, mountain biking, and off-roading adventures, or explore the wilderness on your own. After a soak, visitors can explore nearby Nathrop, Buena Vista, and Salida for shopping, dining, or a drink at one of the local breweries.

Best Time to Visit: Summer is the busiest time of year, but fall and spring are also great times to visit.

Pass/Permit/Fees: Adults cost $20/$25 and kids cost $15/$20 for weekday/weekend passes. Private hot springs are available for $125–$800.

Closest City or Town: Nathrop

How to Get There: From Nathrop, head south on County Rd. 198 and turn right onto County Rd. 197. In 0.2 miles, turn left onto US-285 S, then take a right onto County Rd. 162/Chalk Creek Dr. In 4.4 miles, take two lefts to reach Mt. Princeton Hot Springs.

GPS Coordinates: 38.7329° N, 106.1617° W

Did You Know? One of the original hotels at Mount Princeton Hot Springs took nearly four years to build and never saw a single customer.

Rifle Falls State Park

Ready to explore some caves? The hiking trail around the 70-foot waterfalls at Rifle Falls State Park is surrounded by caves and caverns. Bring a flashlight and be prepared to crawl on your hands and knees for a little extra adventure. Coyote Trail is a 1.5-mile round trip that leads visitors to the base of the falls and around the caves before heading upwards towards the view atop Rifle Falls. Explore the park further by taking Bobcat Trail to the park's fish hatchery or following Squirrel Trail to the campgrounds. The falls themselves are a sight to cherish. The water forks off into three separate waterfalls, creating a sheet of mist that breeds a beautiful mix of flora along the rocks. In the winter, the falls freeze into a naturally beautiful ice sculpture.

Best Time to Visit: Spring and summer are best. Come as soon as the park opens at 7 a.m. to avoid crowded trails.

Pass/Permit/Fees: $9 per vehicle, $4 per pedestrian, $80 annual pass

Closest City or Town: New Castle

How to Get There: From New Castle, follow Country Rd. 245 and County Rd. 226 to CO-325 N. Turn right onto CO-325 N, and the park will be on the right in 2.7 miles at 5775 Highway 325.

GPS Coordinates: 39.6742° N, -107.6992° W

Did You Know? Before it was a state park, Rifle Falls was home to the state's first hydroelectric power plants.

Box Canyon Falls

Get a taste of Switzerland in Colorado at Box Canyon Falls. The 285-foot waterfall drops thousands of gallons of water every minute, and visitors should dress for the mist. The half-mile path to the falls leads to a suspension bridge across the gorge.

Picnic areas and hiking trails of various skill levels are scattered nearby, and while dogs aren't allowed on the path to the falls, they are welcome on the surrounding trails. The High Bridge Trail loops 200 feet up with a stellar view of the Amphitheater Cirque, and the Native Plant Loop leads hikers on an easy trail through wildflowers and plants.

In the summer, keep an eye out for the black swift bird that nests in the canyon. This feathered friend is a rarity, and it's a treat to see them soaring around the falls.

Best Time to Visit: March through November

Pass/Permit/Fees: $5 per person

Closest City or Town: Ouray

How to Get There: In Ouray, take 6th Ave. to 2nd St. Turn right onto 3rd Ave., and take a slight left to reach the park at 30 Box Canyon Rd.

GPS Coordinates: 38.0177° N, -107.6740° W

Did You Know? The mine at Box Canyon established Ouray as a permanent city.

Orvis Hot Springs

Soak up the view of the San Juan Mountains while soaking it up in the hot springs. Orvis Hot Springs Resort offers seven different hot springs that range in temperature from 98–112°F and depths of 2–5 feet. The biggest hot spring, known as The Pond, is 40 feet wide with a 5-foot depth, but the smaller Smoker's Pond comes with its very own waterfall. If you really want to cook, take a dip in the Lobster Pond, which can reach 114°F.

Nearly all of the hot springs are outdoors, except for one indoor pool and two private hot tubs. Orvis Hot Springs is a family-friendly resort, but the hot springs are clothing optional, and pets are not allowed. Campsites are available for tents and RVs.

Best Time to Visit: In spring and winter, the hot springs provide a reprieve from the cold.

Pass/Permit/Fees: $22 per adult, $10 for children under 12

Closest City or Town: Ouray

How to Get There: From Ouray, head north on US-550 N/3rd St./Main St. toward 7th Avenue. In 8.7 miles, turn left onto County Rd. 3, and you'll arrive at the springs at 1585 County Rd. 3.

GPS Coordinates: 38.1338° N, -107.7351° W

Did You Know? The hottest water at Orvis is in The Crater pool, keeping it a balmy 127°F. No one soaks in this hot spring, but the hot water is used to heat the resort buildings, showers, and the other pools during the winter.

Ouray Ice Park

Ouray Ice Park has over 100 man-made ice climbs across the canyon of Uncompahgre Gorge, with 3 miles of vertical terrain and 11 separate climbing areas. The park creates the ice structures starting in November, but the first few months of the year are the best times to climb. For families, the park offers climbing clinics for kids ages 7–17 on the first Saturdays in January, February, and March.

Otherwise, Ouray Ice Park does not offer guided climbs or adult lessons. Nearby outfitters in Ouray do provide equipment and supplies, and the park has a list of helpful guides who teach courses and lead climbs if needed. After an icy climb, the city of Ouray offers five different hot springs to warm up, the largest of which is the Ouray Hot Springs pool facility.

Best Time to Visit: January through March. The annual Ice Festival happens in January.

Pass/Permit/Fees: Ouray Ice Park is free, but donations are accepted.

Closest City or Town: Ouray

How to Get There: From Ouray, head south on US-550 S for 0.6 miles. Turn right onto State Hwy. 361/Camp Bird Rd., and in 0.3 miles you'll reach the park at 280 County Rd. 361.

GPS Coordinates: 38.0145° N, -107.6717° W

Did You Know? Ouray Ice Park is the first ice-climbing park in the world.

Ridgway State Park

Ridgway State Park is tucked up against the entrance of the San Juan Mountain Range. Pick from one of the park's 14 miles of hiking trails, or get out on your boat and hit the reservoir. Two of the most popular hiking trails in Ridgeway are along the water, with the Uncompahgre Riverwalk being the easier of the two. The 7-mile Ridgway Reservoir Trail is grittier and narrower, making it less accessible for wheelchairs and younger hikers.

Drive-up and walk-up campsites and yurts are available by reservation only, and there are picnic spots scattered throughout the park. Summer is the perfect time to enjoy the water, but winter months mean fewer crowds and a better view of the San Juan Mountains.

Best Time to Visit: Summer is excellent for water sports, but there's definitely a crowd. Visiting during the winter months truly captures the essence of the icy peaks.

Pass/Permit/Fees: $9 per vehicle, $80 annual pass, $18–$41 to camp, $60–$90 for yurts

Closest City or Town: Ouray

How to Get There: From Ouray, follow US-550 N toward 7th Ave. Follow for 14.3 miles, and you'll find the park at 28555 Highway 550.

GPS Coordinates: 38.2292° N, -107.7470° W

Did You Know? Bears are commonly seen in the area. Stay safe and follow bear camping protocols.

The Million Dollar Highway

What began as a narrow wagon road in 1882 is now one of the most scenic—and dangerous—drives in Colorado. The driver will have to keep their eyes on the road, but passengers can soak in the views of the San Juan Mountains from the very edge of their seat.

At its simplest, the Million Dollar Highway is a stretch of US-550 through Silverton and Ouray. It was carved into the side of a mountain to create a path for the silver rush, originally costing $10,000 per square mile to build (in case you were wondering how it was named).

It wasn't paved until the 1920s, and even today, a double yellow line does nothing for the nerves when drivers are often sharing this narrow piece of highway with RVs. Don't miss your chance to drive this bit of American history, but do drive at your own risk.

Best Time to Visit: September is best to see how golden the aspen trees become in the fall, or visit late spring after the snow melts to avoid a crowded highway.

Pass/Permit/Fees: None

Closest City or Town: Ouray

How to Get There: From Ouray, head south on US-550 S to enjoy the Million Dollar Highway.

GPS Coordinates: 38.4480° N, -107. 6708° W

Did You Know? In 1882, it cost $5 per cattle head to use the Million Dollar Highway, which would be $125 today.

Blue Mesa Reservoir

Blue Mesa is the largest lake in Colorado and one of three reservoirs that make up the Curecanti National Recreation Area. The reservoir touches the highway, sweeping along the North Rim of Black Canyon. It's surrounded by 96 miles of shoreline that's perfect for picnicking, camping, boating, sailing, fishing, and hiking.

Don't worry about bringing your own equipment. Two marinas, Elk Creek and Lake Fork, can provide boat rentals and repair supplies, bait and tackle, kayaks, and enough souvenirs for the crew back home. Kick off your adventure on a hike through Neversink Trail, an easy 3-mile round trip around the water. The trailhead is wheelchair accessible and perfect for families. For a more intense hike, take the 4-mile trek to Dillon Pinnacles.

Best Time to Visit: May through September. Take advantage of ranger-led hikes from June to September.

Pass/Permit/Fees: None

Closest City or Town: Sapinero

How to Get There: From Sapinero, follow US-50 E for 5.6 miles to reach the Blue Mesa Reservoir.

GPS Coordinates: 38.4729° N, -107.2105° W

Did You Know? The Denver & Rio Grande Western Railroad Scenic Line originally ran through 15 miles of Curecanti, and you can still spot remnants of the track.

Wheeler Geologic Area

This geologic wonderland in the middle of the San Juan Mountains is one of the most remote and serene spots in Colorado. There are no hotels, restaurants, crowds, hot springs, or ski resorts. The only way to access Wheeler is either on foot via the 7-mile East Bellows Trailhead or on a grueling 14-mile route that requires four-wheel drive. The Wheeler Geologic Area was formed by layers of volcanic ash that have eroded over the centuries, leaving behind unique hoodoos and spires that look like gnome or fairy homes. Add to the magical element of the area by hiking in late summer for a beautiful view of the wildflowers, or explore further into the La Garita Wilderness off any of the nearby hiking trails.

Best Time to Visit: June through September. Wheeler is open all year round, but winter weather will limit access.

Pass/Permit/Fees: None

Closest City or Town: South Fork

How to Get There: To get to the East Bellows Trailhead from South Fork, head west on CO-149 N toward CO-149 S. In 14 miles, turn right onto Pool Table Rd./US First Service Rd. 600. You'll arrive at East Bellows Creek in 8.8 miles, and it's a 7-mile hike to the geologic area. A four-wheeler is recommended if not hiking the trail.

GPS Coordinates: 37.8839° N, -106.7837° W

Did You Know? The area is named for Captain George M. Wheeler, who surveyed the area in 1874.

Fish Creek Falls

Hikers have their choice when it comes to seeing the 280-foot-tall Fish Creek Falls. Two quick quarter-mile trails lead you to an excellent view of the lower falls, including the Fish Creek Falls Overlook trail, which is wheelchair accessible. Take a 5-mile round trip from the base of Fish Creek Falls to a second (often overlooked) waterfall, or turn it into a day trip with a 13-mile round trip to Upper Fish Creek Falls and Long Lake. This trail brings hikers deeper into the heart of the Routt National Forest for picnics and sweeping views of nature.

Come in the spring to see the snowmelt roar off the falls, or brave it in the winter for an epic ice climb. Even if there isn't an ice climber in your group, it is a sight to see others scale the frozen falls as you hike around the base of Fish Creek.

Best Time to Visit: May through September. Bring snowshoes in the spring and winter to hike in the snow.

Pass/Permit/Fees: Free to hike, $5 to park

Closest City or Town: Steamboat Springs

How to Get There: From Steamboat Springs, head northeast on 6th St. At the first cross street, turn right onto Oak St. Turn left onto Fish Creek Falls Rd/Rcr 32, and you'll reach the falls in 0.7 miles.

GPS Coordinates: 40.4816° N, -106.7712° W

Did You Know? Over 25 feet of snow can cover the falls during the winter.

114

Strawberry Park Natural Hot Springs

With over 40 acres of hot springs, Strawberry Park is one of the warmest and most minimalistic places in Colorado. Each cabin is made with either wood or stone to blend in with the mountain valley, and you better bring a flashlight if you plan on staying overnight—there are not many artificial lights to lead your way. Overnight stays are reserved for adults only. After sunset, clothing is optional, and minors are not allowed in the hot springs. Hikers can take their choice of day hikes on the Lower Bear and Hot Springs Trailheads. Lower Bear Trailhead leads to campsites just a quarter mile away, or you can take Buffalo Pass Road to the campgrounds farther out.

Best Time to Visit: May through October. Only vehicles with four-wheel drive are allowed at the springs from November 1 until the end of April.

Pass/Permit/Fees: $20 per person

Closest City or Town: Steamboat Springs

How to Get There: From Steamboat Springs, head northeast on 6th St. toward Oak St. Continue onto Laurel St. and then Park Ave. Turn left onto N. Park Rd. and then take a right onto Strawberry Park Rd. Turn left onto County Rd. 36/Rcr 36, and follow until you reach the springs at 44200 County Rd. 36.

GPS Coordinates: 40.5598° N, -106.8494° W

Did You Know? The icy creek flowing through the middle of the springs helps regulate the hot springs with its cool max temperature of 40°F.

Blue Lakes

Blue Lakes is the star of Mount Sneffels Wilderness in the Uncompahgre National Forest. To reach them, take the Blue Lakes trailhead and veer right when the path forks off. You'll know you're close to the lake when you pass a rocky waterfall on your left. The hiking trails at Blue Lakes are steep and rugged, and it can take over 2–3 hours to reach Lower Blue Lake. Visiting before the summer months means being prepared for sudden snowfall. These trails showcase the wildflowers that bloom in this area during the summer, but only experienced climbers should continue up to the Mt. Sneffels summit.

Best Time to Visit: Mid-July through August is the best time to see the wildflowers bloom.

Pass/Permit/Fees: $12 per vehicle to enter Brainard Lake Recreation Area

Closest City or Town: Telluride

How to Get There: From Telluride, head west on W. Colorado Ave, and then at the traffic circle, continue straight onto W. 145 Spur Hwy./CO-145. In 2.9 miles, take the first exit at the traffic circle onto CO-145 N. Turn right onto CO-62 E/State Hwy. 62 in 12.7 miles. In 18.5 miles, turn right onto County Rd. 7. Keep right to stay on County Rd. 7, and you will reach the Blue Lakes Trailhead.

GPS Coordinates: 38.03728° N, -107.80688° W

Did You Know? Mount Sneffels is named for Snæfell, an Icelandic volcano featured in Jules Verne's *Journey to the Center of the Earth.*

Bridal Veil Falls

Bridal Veil Falls is a hidden gem that hikers can reach from a trail that starts right downtown. Follow the 1.8-mile path up to the Bridal Veil Basin, then continue upward for a view atop the falls. This beautiful hike is rich in wildflowers, wildlife, and picturesque views. Visitors can drive about 20 minutes outside of downtown Telluride to reach the falls. This mist is heavy at the base, so the best photo ops are at the top. Vehicles are not permitted beyond the top of the falls, but hikers can explore past the gate for views of the Bridal Veil Canyon and Blue Lake. During the winter, access to the falls may be limited, but ice climbing is very popular. The falls are considered one of the most difficult ice climbs in the country, and only experienced rock climbers should attempt it.

Best Time to Visit: Spring, when snowmelt is at its peak, is the best time to see the falls.

Pass/Permit/Fees: $25 per vehicle, $15 per pedestrian

Closest City or Town: Telluride

How to Get There: From Telluride, head east on W. Colorado Ave toward S. Fir St. Next, W. Colorado turns slightly right and becomes Forest Service Rd. 648. Continue straight onto Black Bear Pass Summit, and follow for 0.8 miles to the falls.

GPS Coordinates: 37.9191° N, -107.7700° W

Did You Know? The summit of Bridal Veil Falls was first reached when climbers Jeff Lowe and Mike Weiss made it to the top in 1978.

Ophir Valley

Ophir Valley is a tiny former mining town tucked away between the 13,000 peaks of the San Juan Mountains. The nearby Ophir Pass Road is a scenic 6 miles over a 12,789-foot summit to Red Mountain Pass. It's a rather difficult off-road trail, so a proper vehicle is required. By foot, take the Lizard Head Trail off Highway 145. This 18-mile hike forks into Wilson Meadows Trail after the first 3.5 miles. The town has strict Leave No Trace policies, and you must respect nature and wildlife when visiting any of the nearby lakes and hiking trails. Much of the town shuts down in winter due to weather-related road closures and avalanche risks, but experienced travelers and hikers can enjoy cross-country skiing and snowshoeing.

Best Time to Visit: June through October is best since that's when Ophir Pass is open. Most roads through the valley are closed during the winter.

Pass/Permit/Fees: There is no fee.

Closest City or Town: Telluride

How to Get There: From Telluride, head south on Highway 145. In 8 miles, take the Old Ophir Pass Road to Ophir Pass.

GPS Coordinates: 37.8569392° N, -107.8325644° W

Did You Know? In 2010, the Trust for Public Land successfully campaigned for the protection and preservation of Ophir Valley and some 9,000 acres surrounding the town.

Telluride Mountain Village Gondola

The views you'll catch when you ride the "G" are absolutely stunning and absolutely free. It costs nothing to catch a ride down to Mountain Village, and your seat will offer up breathtaking 360-degree views of the San Juan Mountains at over 10,000 feet. The gondola was designed to reduce traffic between the two resort cities. What originally took 20 minutes to drive is now a 13-minute flight above the cities, with sights as far as the La Sal Mountain Range in Utah. During the winter, the city opens up the Chondola to accommodate the number of skiers and snowboarders who flock to the resort. The Chondola is a smaller version of the gondola, with seats for 4. Public riders are free, but skiers will need a lift ticket.

Best Time to Visit: June, July, and August are the best times to ride the gondola and take advantage of Telluride's summer lineup of events.

Pass/Permit/Fees: Free gondola rides are available from June through August.

Closest City or Town: Telluride

How to Get There: In Telluride, head east on W. Colorado Ave. to get to S. Fir St. From S Fir St., take a right onto W. San Juan Ave., and Telluride Station is on the left.

GPS Coordinates: 37.9361° N, -107.8139° W

Did You Know? The Telluride Mountain Village Gondola is the first and only free public transportation of its kind currently in the United States.

Piney Lake

Despite the summer crowds, Piney Lake's remote location makes it one of the most serene spots in Colorado that's also close to a ski resort. The secluded spot offers amenities, including a restaurant, gift shop, and a boathouse to rent canoes, kayaks, and paddleboards. Capture views of the Gore and Rocky mountain ranges on the Upper Piney Trail, a 14-mile round trip with a waterfall halfway through. The trail continues past Knee Knocker Pass. The secret to the lake is staying overnight in a cabin that lines the shore. Piney Lake is closed to the public between 5 p.m. and 10 a.m., making overnight stays a more intimate experience.

Best Time to Visit: Piney River Ranch is only open seasonally from June 21 through September.

Pass/Permit/Fees: A fishing license is required for fishing.

Closest City or Town: Vail

How to Get There: From Vail Ski Resort, head northwest on Vail Valley Dr. toward Chalet Rd. Turn left onto S. Frontage Rd. E. At the traffic circle, take the second exit onto Vail Rd. At the next traffic circle, take the second exit onto N. Frontage Rd. W (I-70). Turn right onto Red Sandstone Rd. Continue onto Piney Lake Rd. This turns into Piney River Rd. The trailhead will be on the left-hand side in about 4 miles.

GPS Coordinates: 39.7205° N, -106.4050° W

Did You Know? Camping is free at Piney Lake, and the best spots are a mile into the park from the road.

Lake Isabelle

Pawnee Pass Trail leads hikers directly to the shores of Lake Isabelle. The 5-mile round trip is very popular, and you will run into crowds exploring the Indian Peaks Wilderness Area during the summer months. The incline is gradual, making it an easy hike for all skill ranges. If you have the time, hike the additional 2 miles on Isabelle Glacier Trail for a unique view of the basin area framed by the three Shoshone, Apache, and Navajo peaks. Be aware that the lake is actually a reservoir and will be drained for agriculture every August, so plan to visit in spring or early summer for the best views. Camping is prohibited at the lake from May through November, but a trip in early spring can mean beautiful views of the water as the snow melts down the mountains.

Best Time to Visit: July through September, or avoid the crowds and visit during the spring

Pass/Permit/Fees: $12 per vehicle from July through October

Closest City or Town: Ward

How to Get There: From Ward, take Utica St. to Nelson, and then turn right onto CO-72 W. In 5.7 miles, turn left onto Brainard Lake Rd., right onto Michell Lake Rd., and then left onto Long Lake Rd. to reach Lake Isabelle.

GPS Coordinates: 40.0694° N, -105.6185° W

Did You Know? This region is designated and protected by the UN as an International Biosphere Reserve for alpine and arctic research.

Proper Planning

With this guide, you are well on your way to properly planning a marvelous adventure. When you plan your travels, you should become familiar with the area, save any maps to your phone for access without internet, and bring plenty of water—especially during the summer months. Depending on the adventure you choose, you will also want to bring snacks and even a lunch. For younger children, you should do your research and find destinations that best suits your family's needs. Additionally, you should also plan when to get gas, local lodgings, and where to get food after you're finished. We've done our best to group these destinations based on nearby towns and cities to help make planning easier.

Dangerous Wildlife

There are several dangerous animals and insects you may encounter while hiking. With a good dose of caution and awareness, you can explore safely. Here is what you can do to keep yourself and your loved ones safe from dangerous flora and fauna while exploring:

- Keep to the established trails.
- Do not look under rocks, leaves, or sticks.
- Keep hands and feet out of small crawl spaces, bushes, covered areas, or crevices.
- Wear long sleeves and pants to keep arms and legs protected.
- Keep your distance should you encounter any dangerous wildlife or plants.

Limited Cell Service

Do not rely on cell service for navigation or emergencies. Always have a map with you and let someone know where you are and for how long you intend to be gone, just in case.

First Aid Information

Always travel with a first aid kit with you in case of emergencies.

Here are items to be certain to include in your primary first aid kit:

- Nitrile gloves
- Blister care products
- Band-aids - multiple sizes and waterproof type
- Ace wrap and athletic tape
- Alcohol wipes and antibiotic ointment
- Irrigation syringe
- Tweezers, nail clippers, trauma shears, safety pins
- Small Ziplock bags containing contaminated trash

It is recommended to also keep a secondary first aid kit, especially when hiking, for more serious injuries or medical emergencies. Items in this should include:

- Blood clotting sponges
- Sterile gauze pads
- Trauma pads
- Second-skin/burn treatment

- Triangular bandages/sling
- Butterfly strips
- Tincture of benzoin
- Medications (ibuprofen, acetaminophen, antihistamine, aspirin, etc.)
- Thermometer
- CPR mask
- Wilderness medicine handbook
- Antivenin

There is so much more to explore, but this is a great start.

For information on all national parks, visit: www.nps.gov.

This site will give you information on up-to-date entrance fees and how to purchase a park pass for unlimited access to national and state parks. This site will also introduce you to all of the trails of each park.

Always check before you travel to destinations to make sure there are no closures. Some hikes close when there is heavy rain or snow in the area, and other parks close parts of their land for the migration of wildlife. Attractions may change their hours or temporarily shut down for various reasons. Check the websites for the most up-to-date information.